ADULTING STINKS:

a sassy adult-ish coloring book

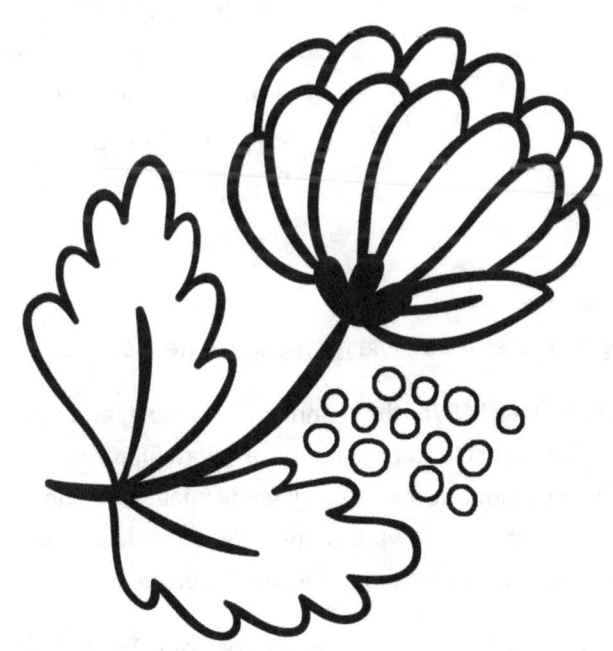

BY FIFI La SWeary

ARTIST'S NOTE

Thank you for buying this book. I hope it helps you cope with difficult days, and if you are going through a tough time, that it brings you many hours of coloring pleasure and relaxation.

This coloring book is the result of many days of adulting. I assembled the pages and cover, digitized every page, then compiled them electronically to prepare a quality book for printing. I have officially registered this book with the Copyright Office. Please respect Copyright Law.

PardonMyColoring.com   Facebook.com/PardonMyFrenchColoring

ISBN-13: 978-1982059750
ISBN-10: 1982059753

THIS BOOK BELONGS TO:

_____

ABOUT THIS BOOK

Who doesn't hate adulting? Some of my fondest childhood memories are not having to pay bills. I made these 30 coloring pages in a variety of styles and levels of complexity to help you cope with those days when you'd rather be in your pillow fort, coloring instead of doing laundry or cleaning the toilet. Six select designs are also in black background for added flair and to color those days when you just don't want to bother staying inside the lines.

The purpose of these coloring pages is to make you chuckle and help you relax and cope. To get the maximum fun out of this book, don't worry about making the final colored pages perfect. This paper is particularly good for coloring pencils, but don't let that limit you. Designs were printed single sided to keep bleed through from ruining the back pages. If you're using markers, slip a couple extra pages or a sheet of cardstock behind the page you're working on so you don't curse because those markers you used bled through to the next image. Most importantly, have fun coloring these pages.

I'd love to see how you color your pages and to hear what they are helping you to cope with. I am also publishing another version of this book along with this one, a sweary version that's there for days when adulting has really got your goat or to give as a gift to your sweary friends and family. I'll be adding many of these designs (both sweary and sassy) to my shop so you can buy them on mugs, stickers, totes, and other items to say adulting stinks on a regular basis. They also make great gifts.

If you have any requests or suggestions for coloring pages, please feel free to find me on Facebook and share them - who knows, you may find I added your page suggestion to my next book - or for instant gratification, to my electronic downloads shop! So visit me at PardonMyColoring.com to see my other books, share your work, get coloring tips, see the shop, and to find out when my next book is out!

À bientôt and happy coloring!

Fifi La Sweary

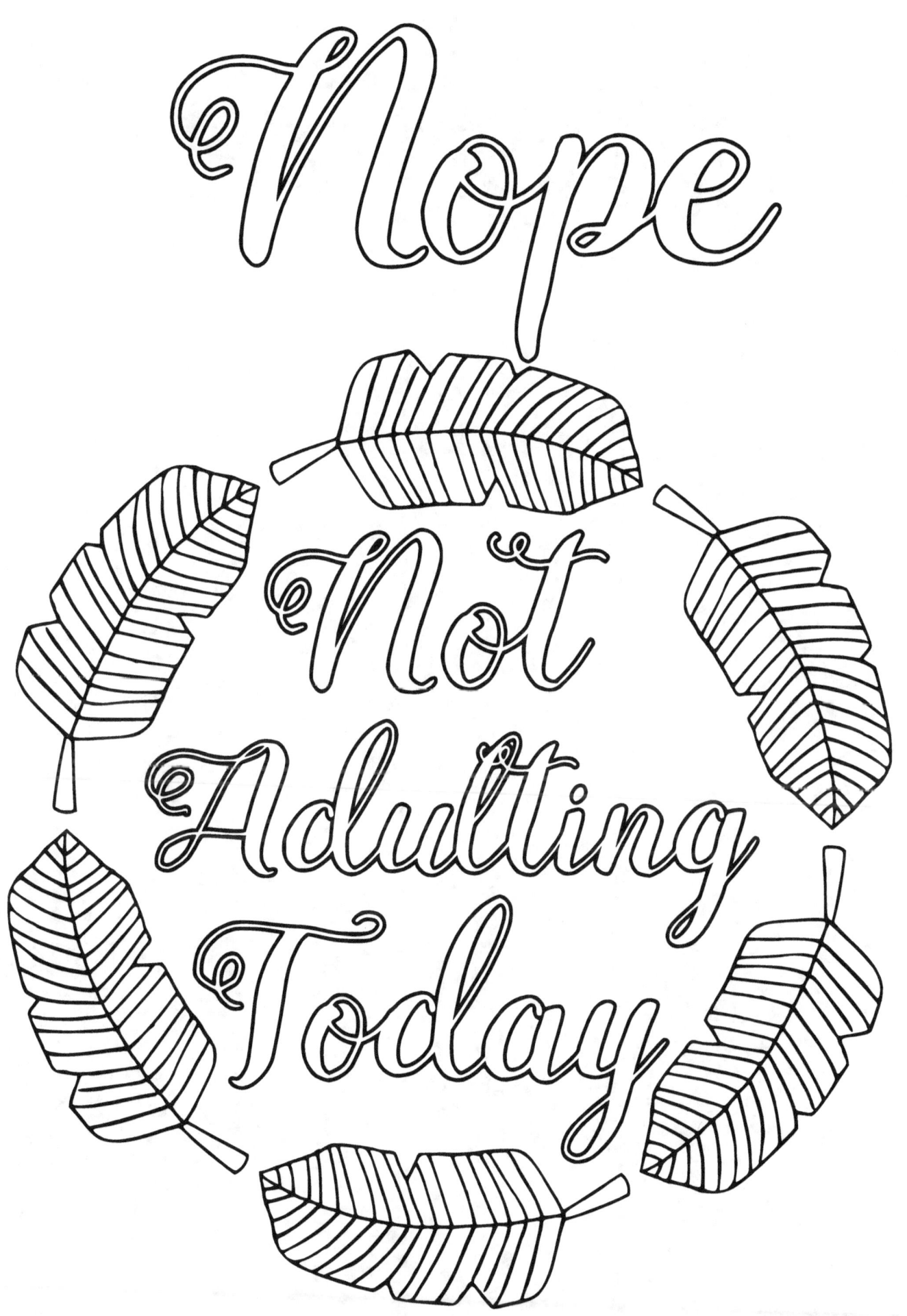

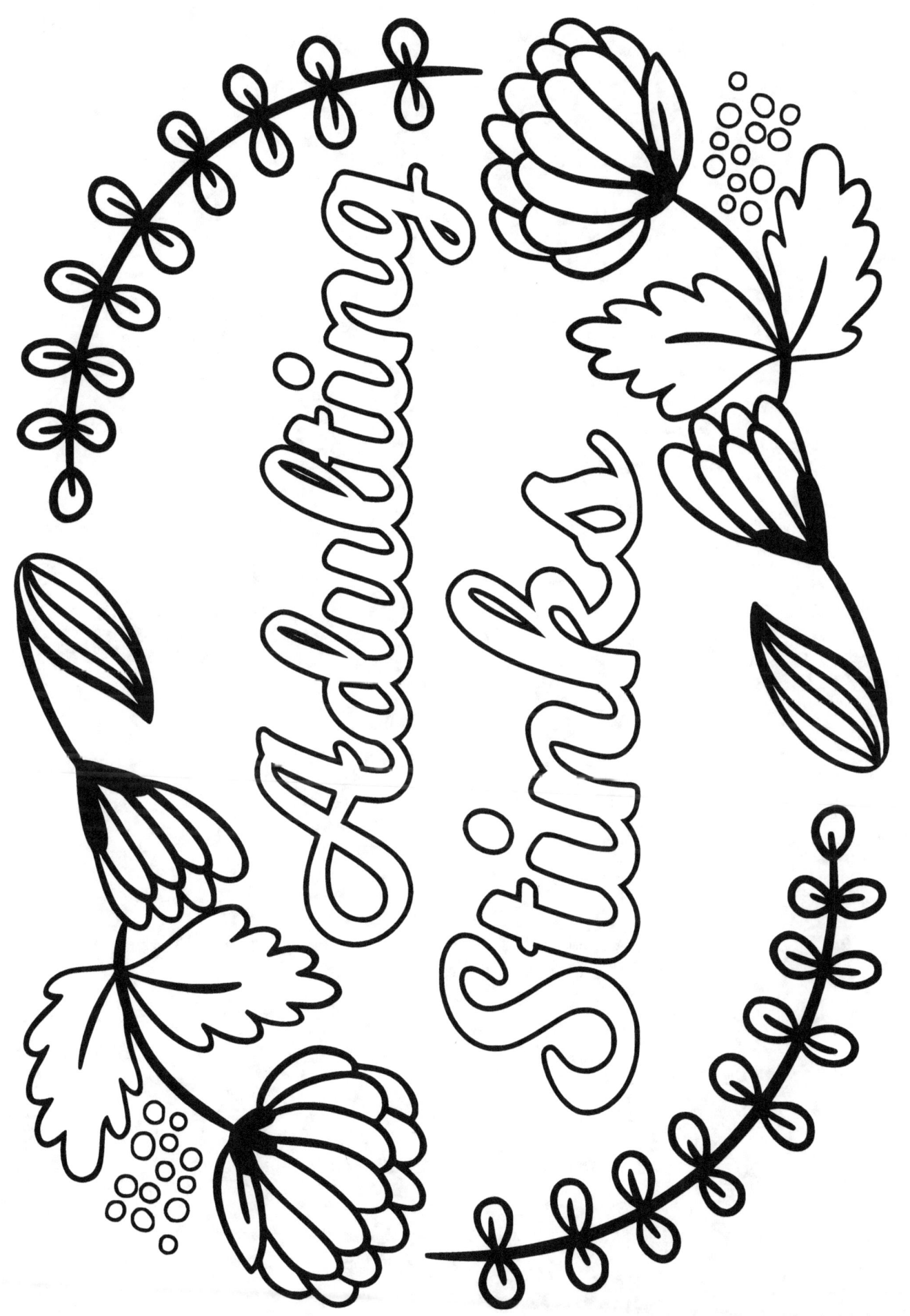

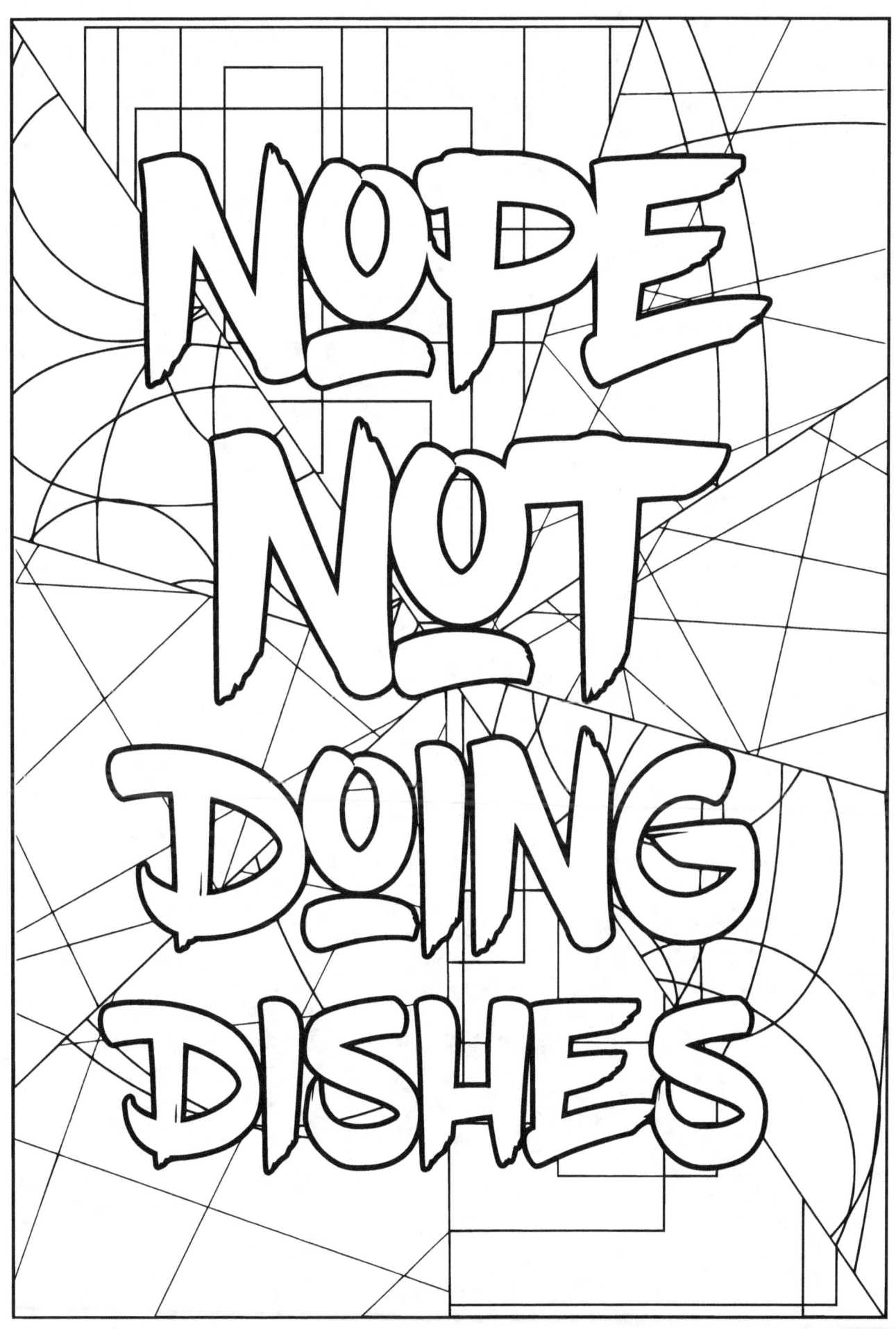

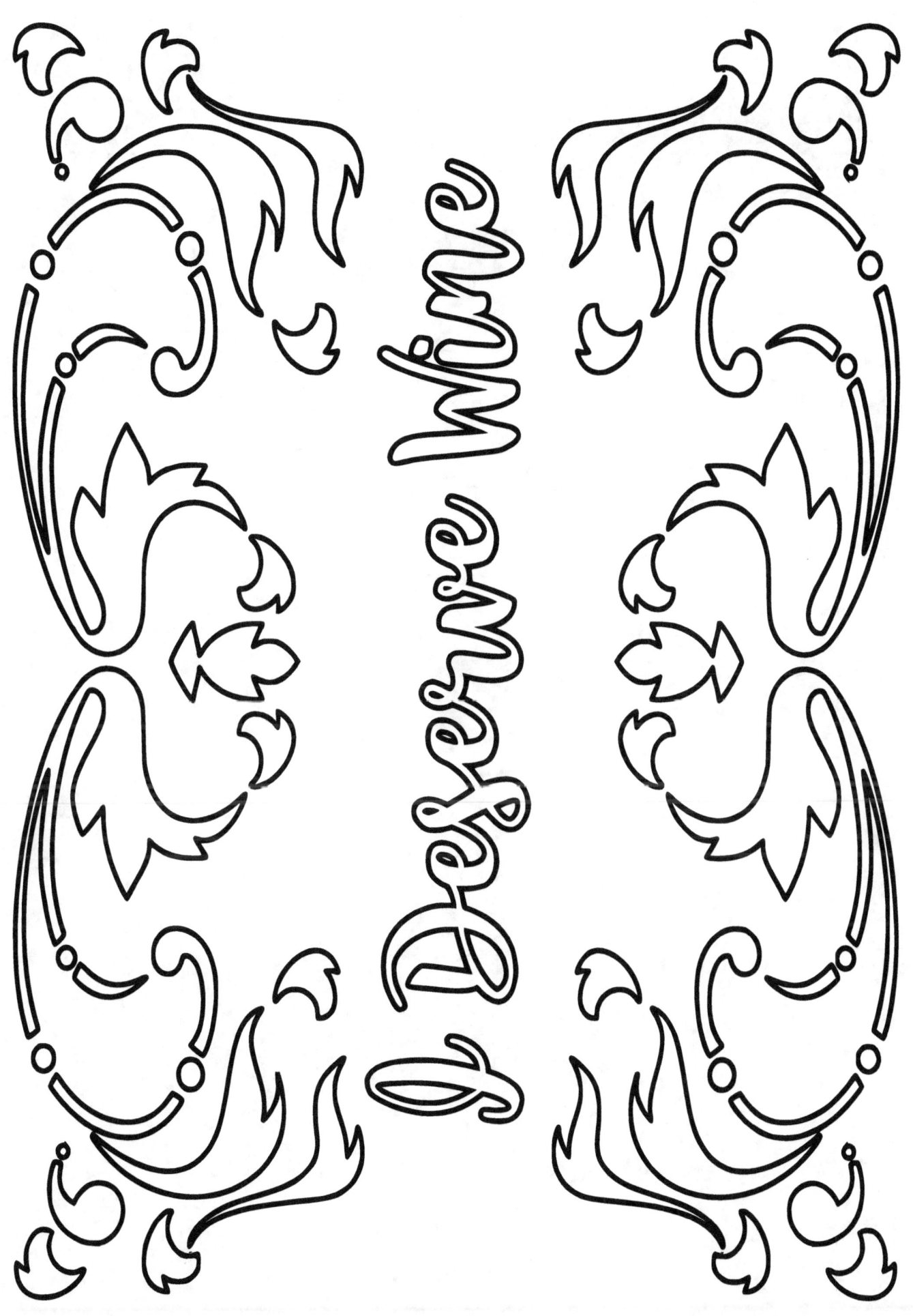

I Deserve Wine

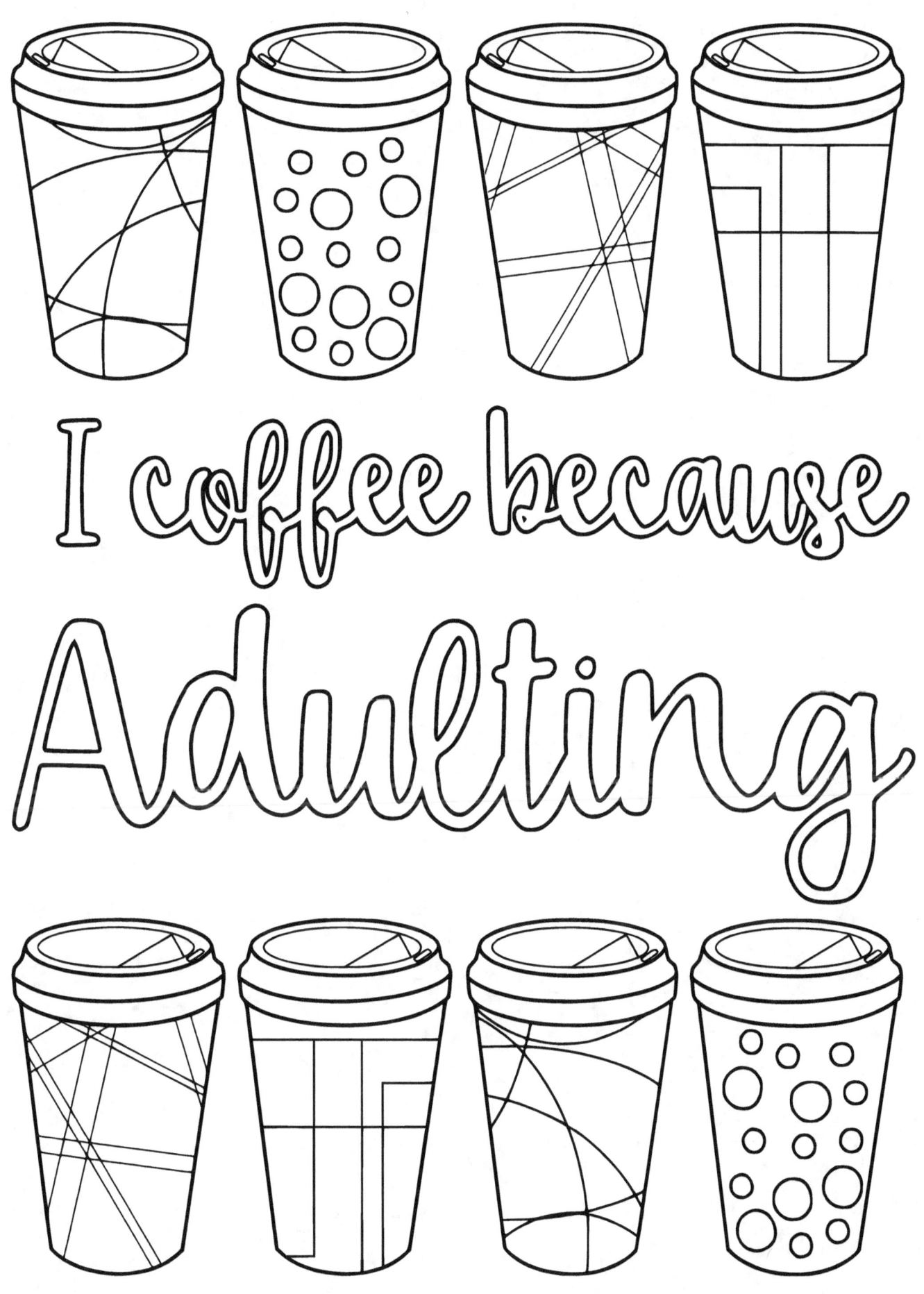

I coffee because Adulting

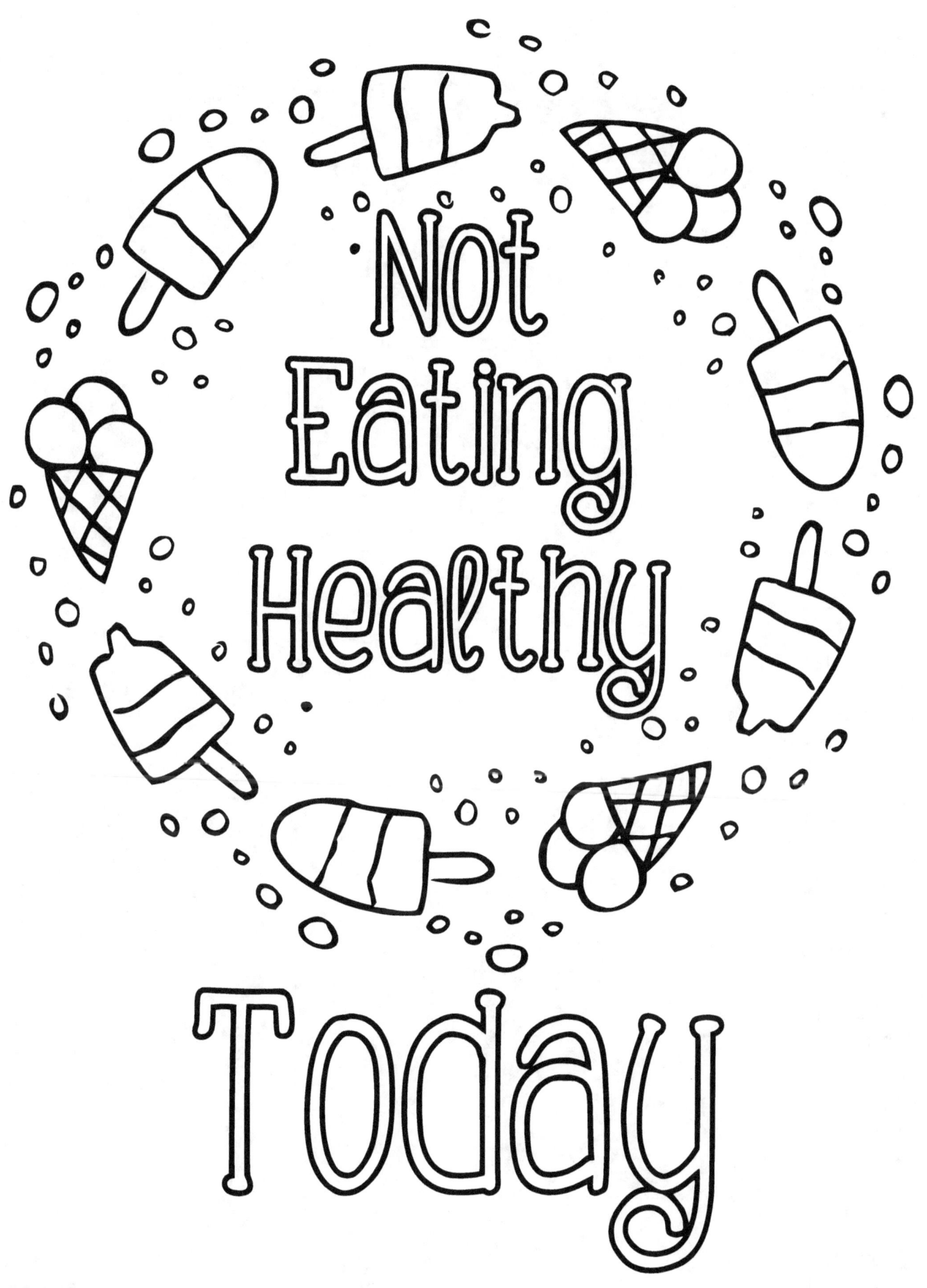

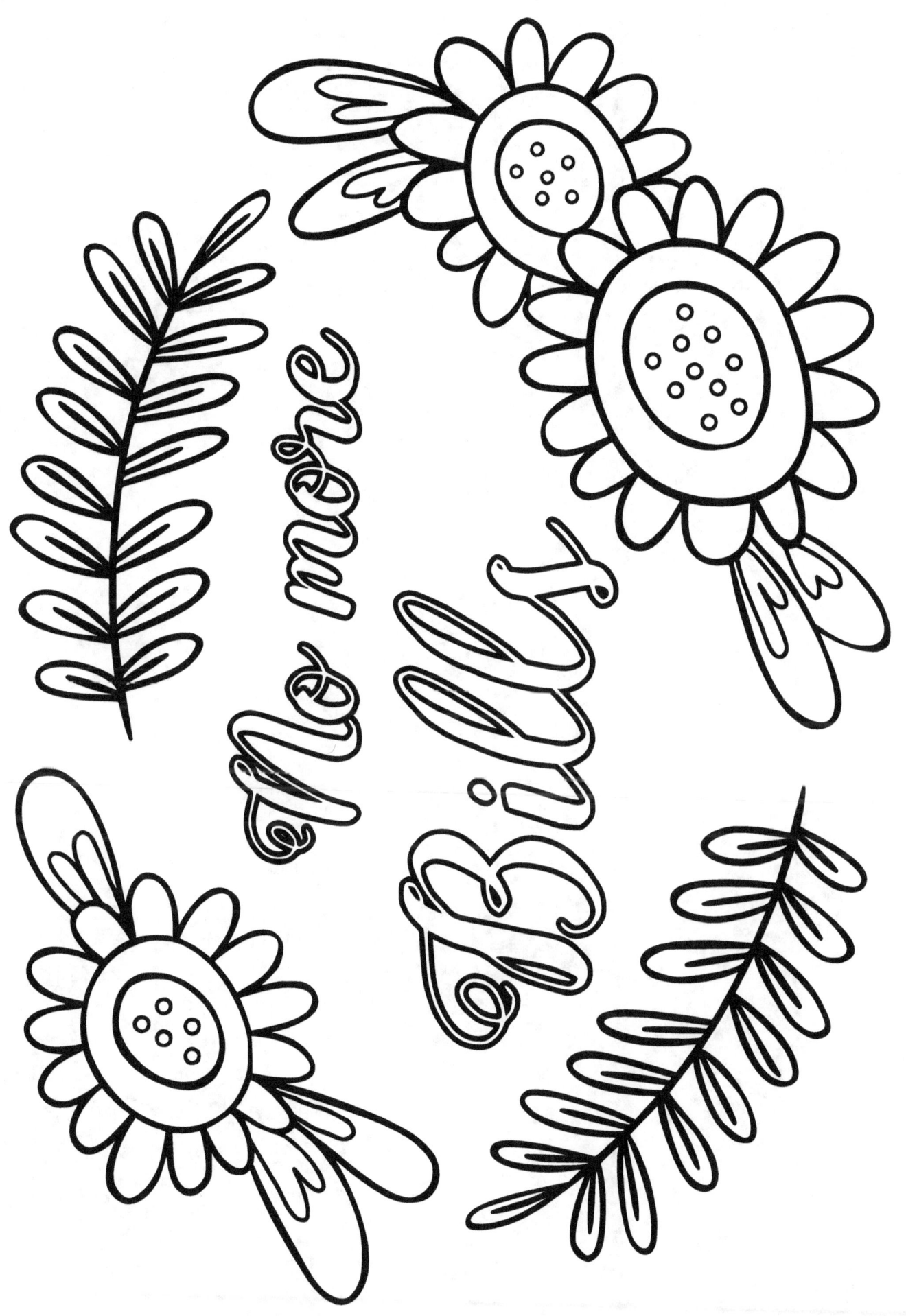

The more Bills

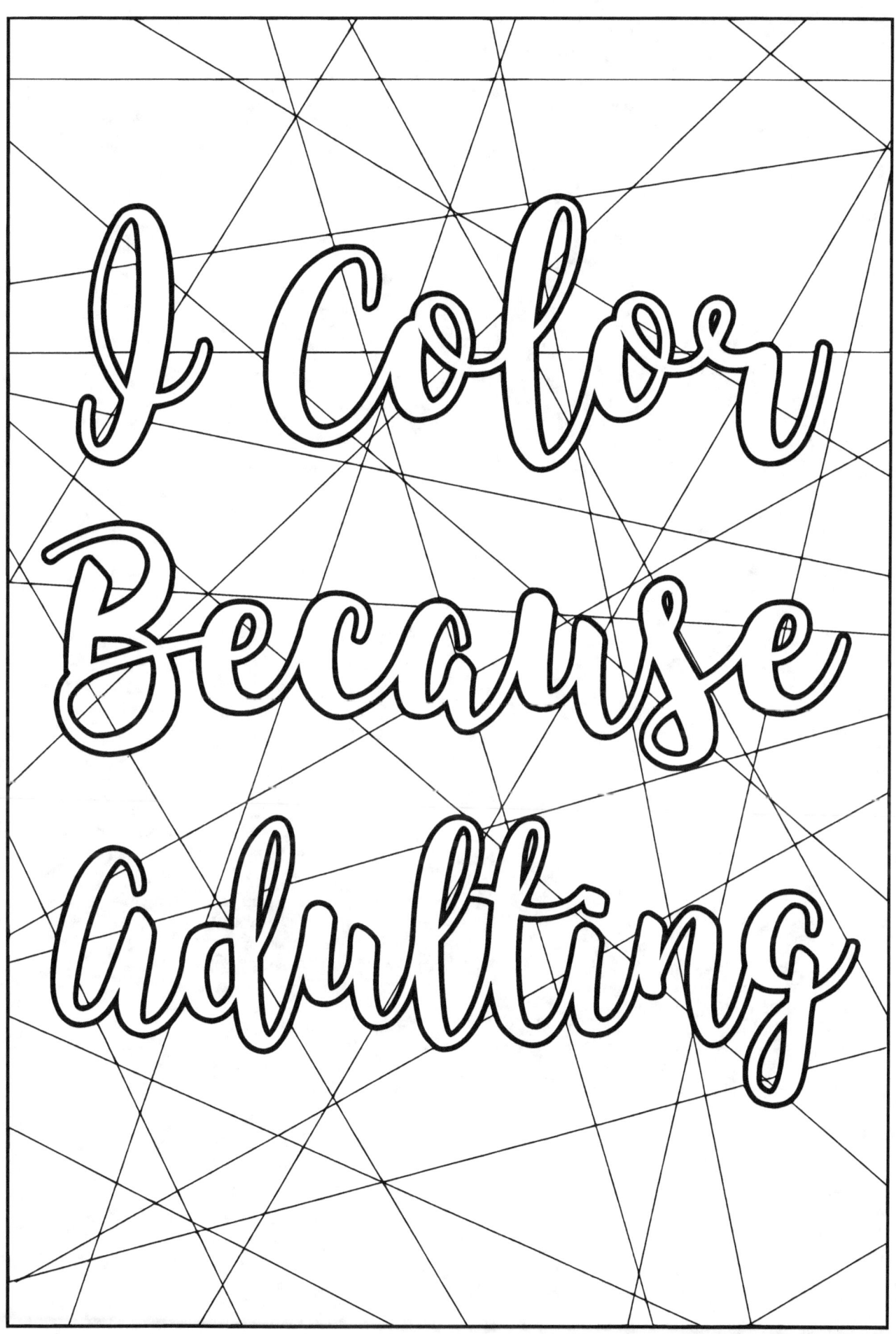

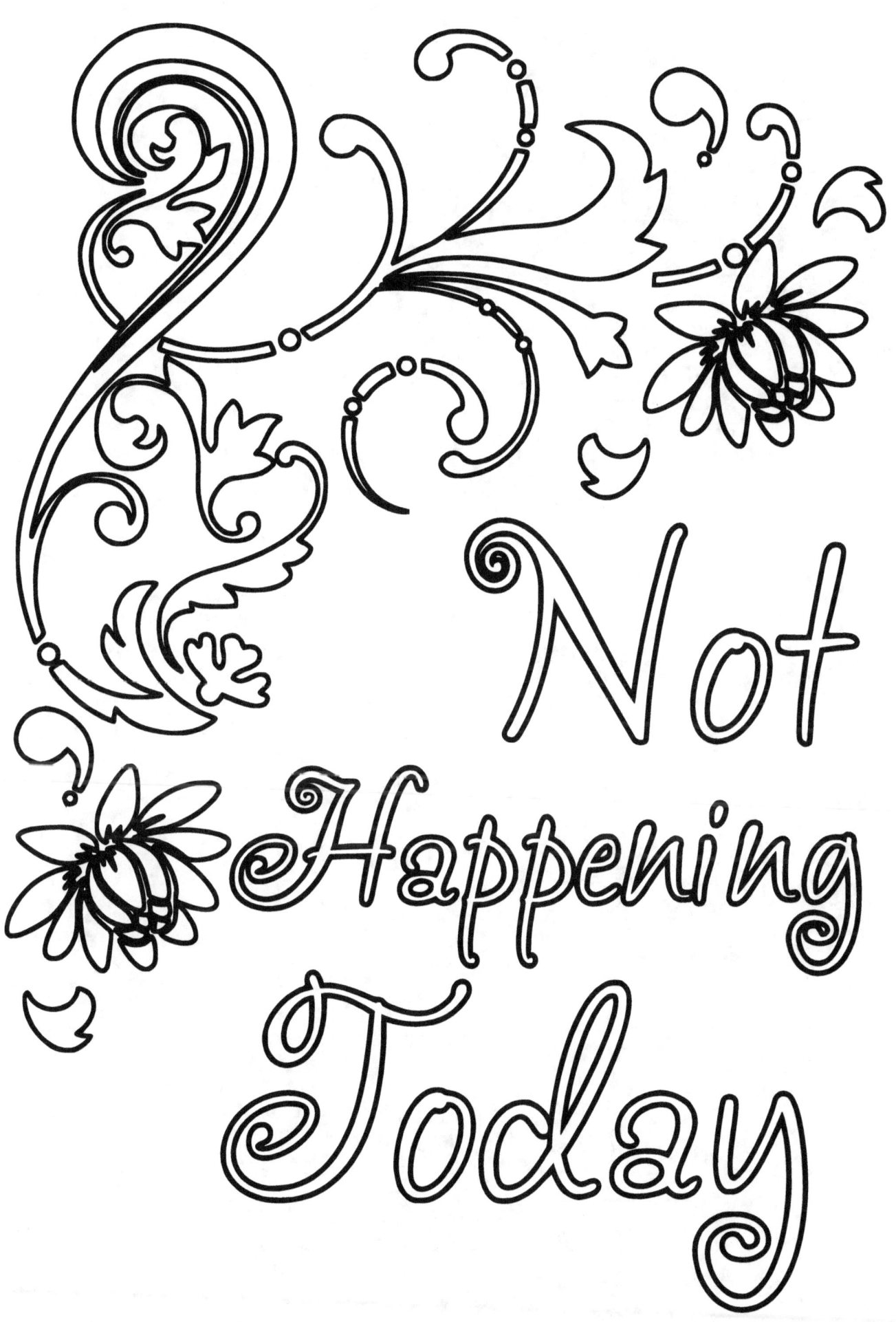

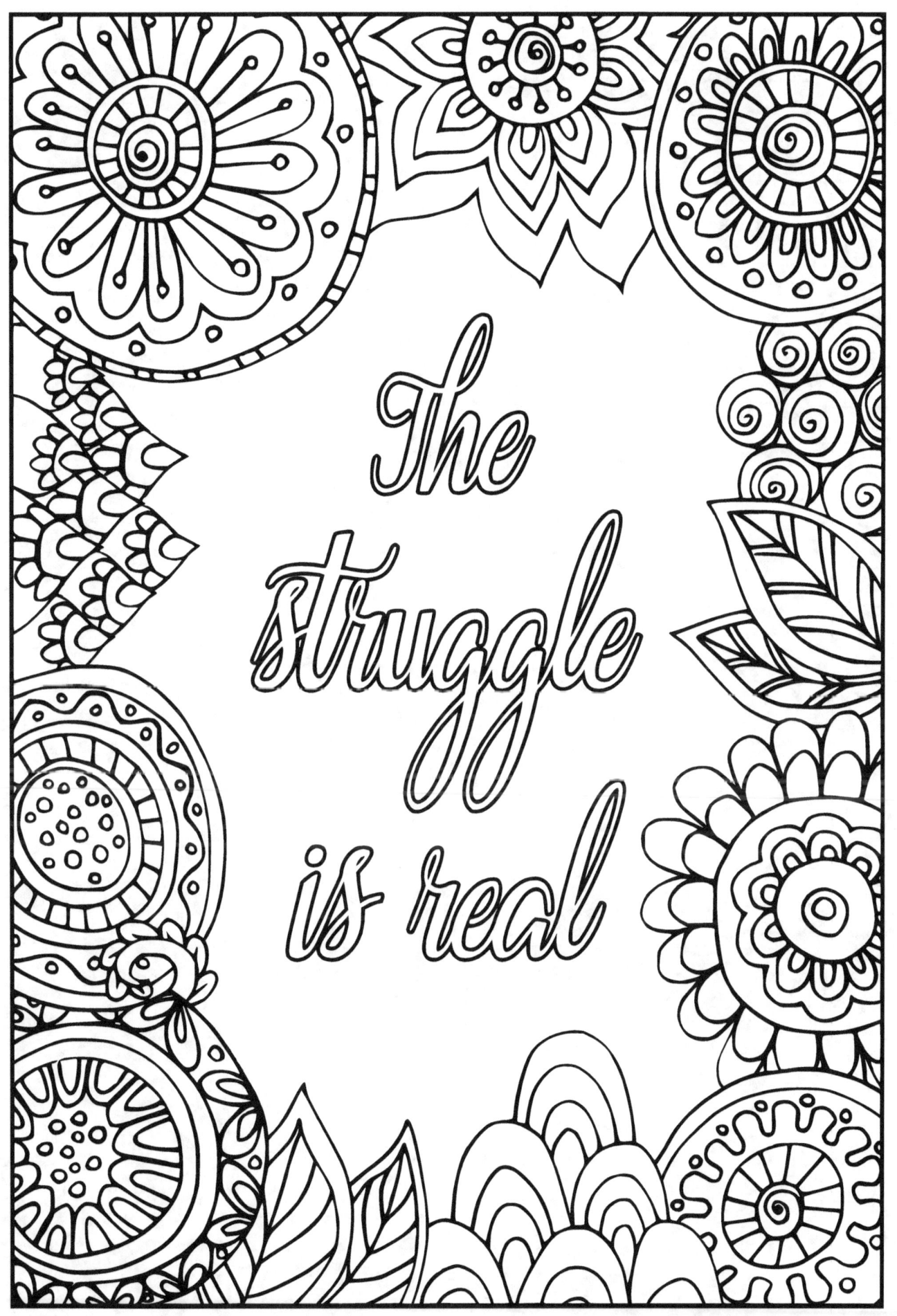

The struggle is real

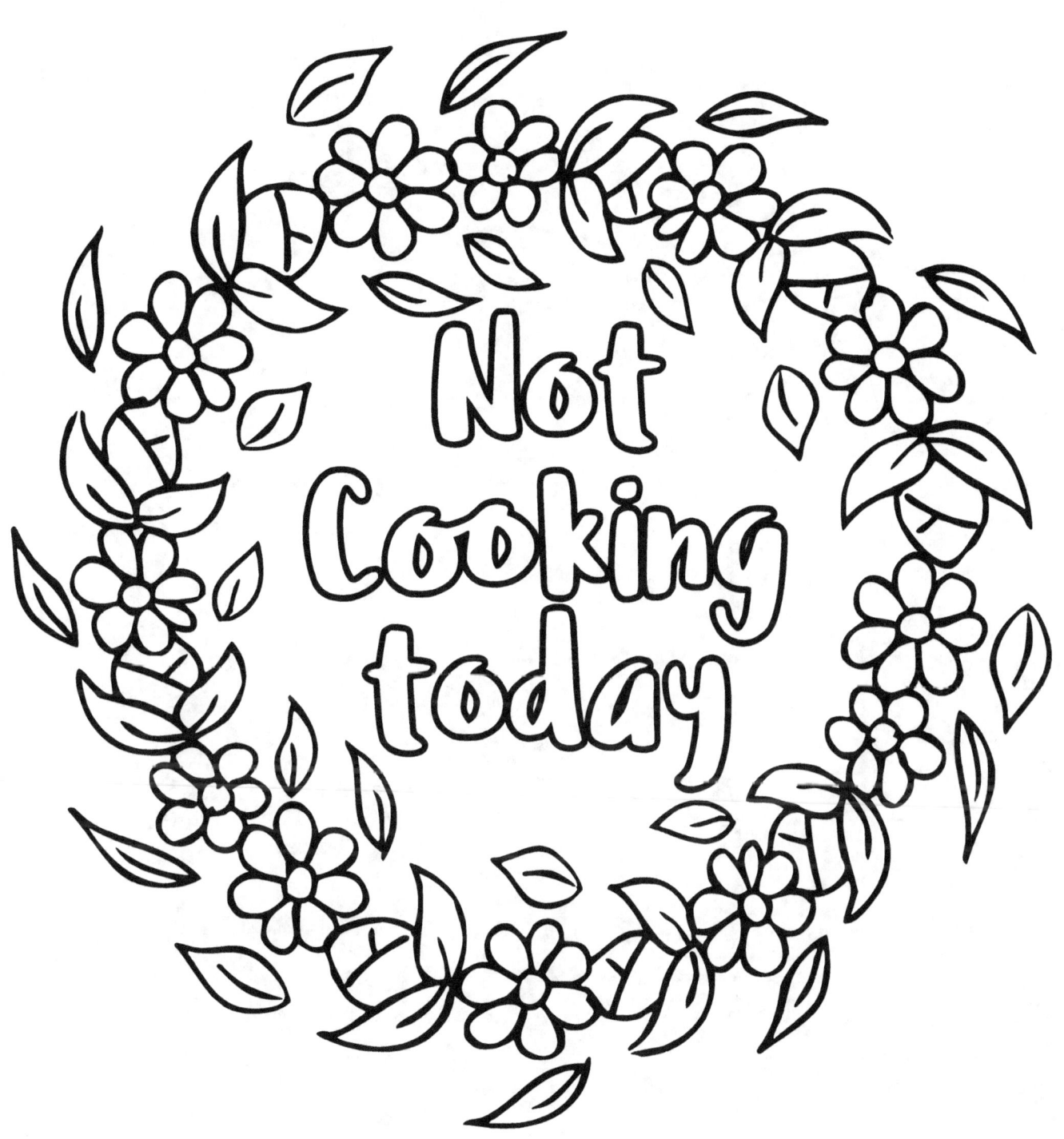

Not Cooking today

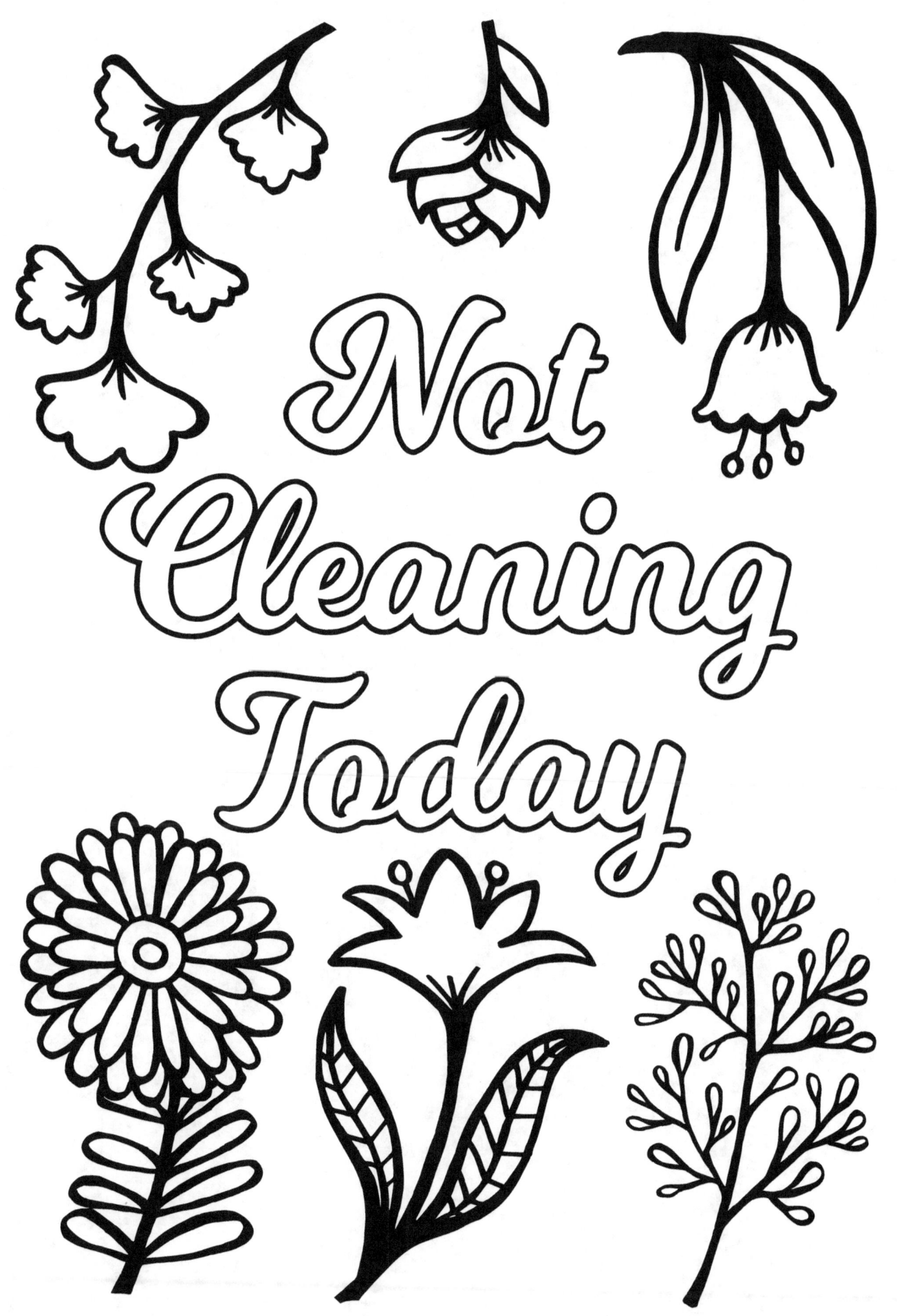

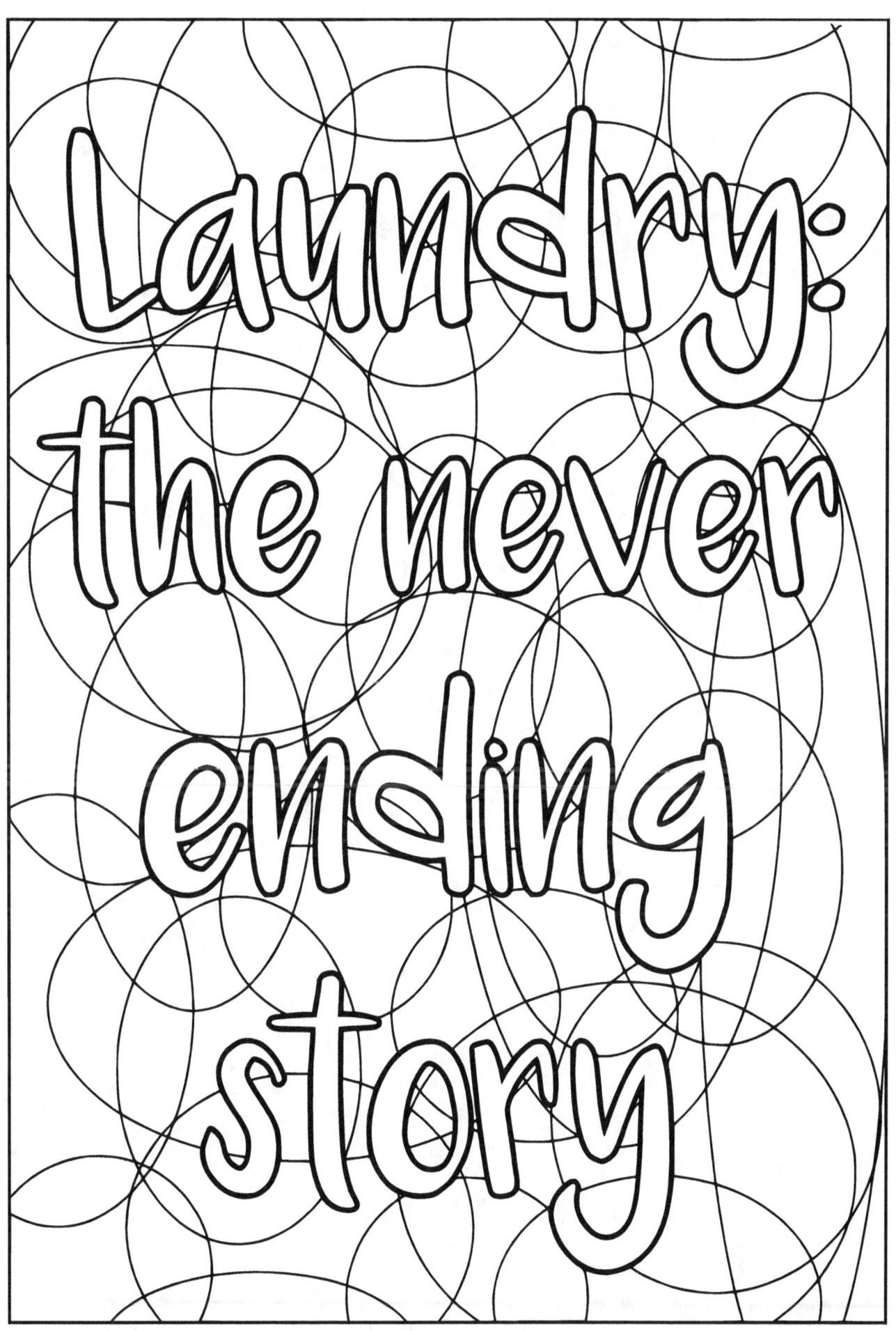

Laundry: the never ending story

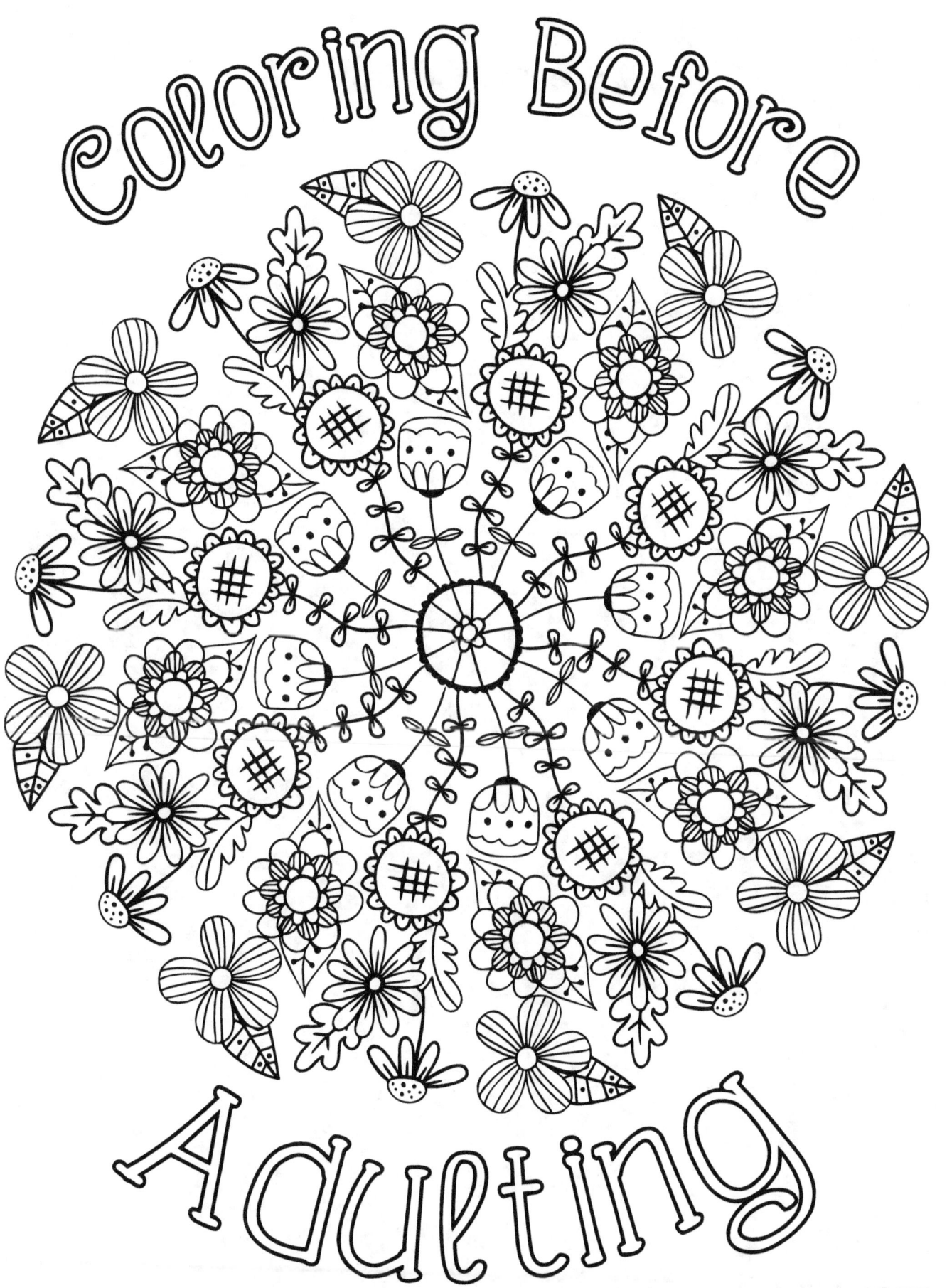

Coloring Before Adulting

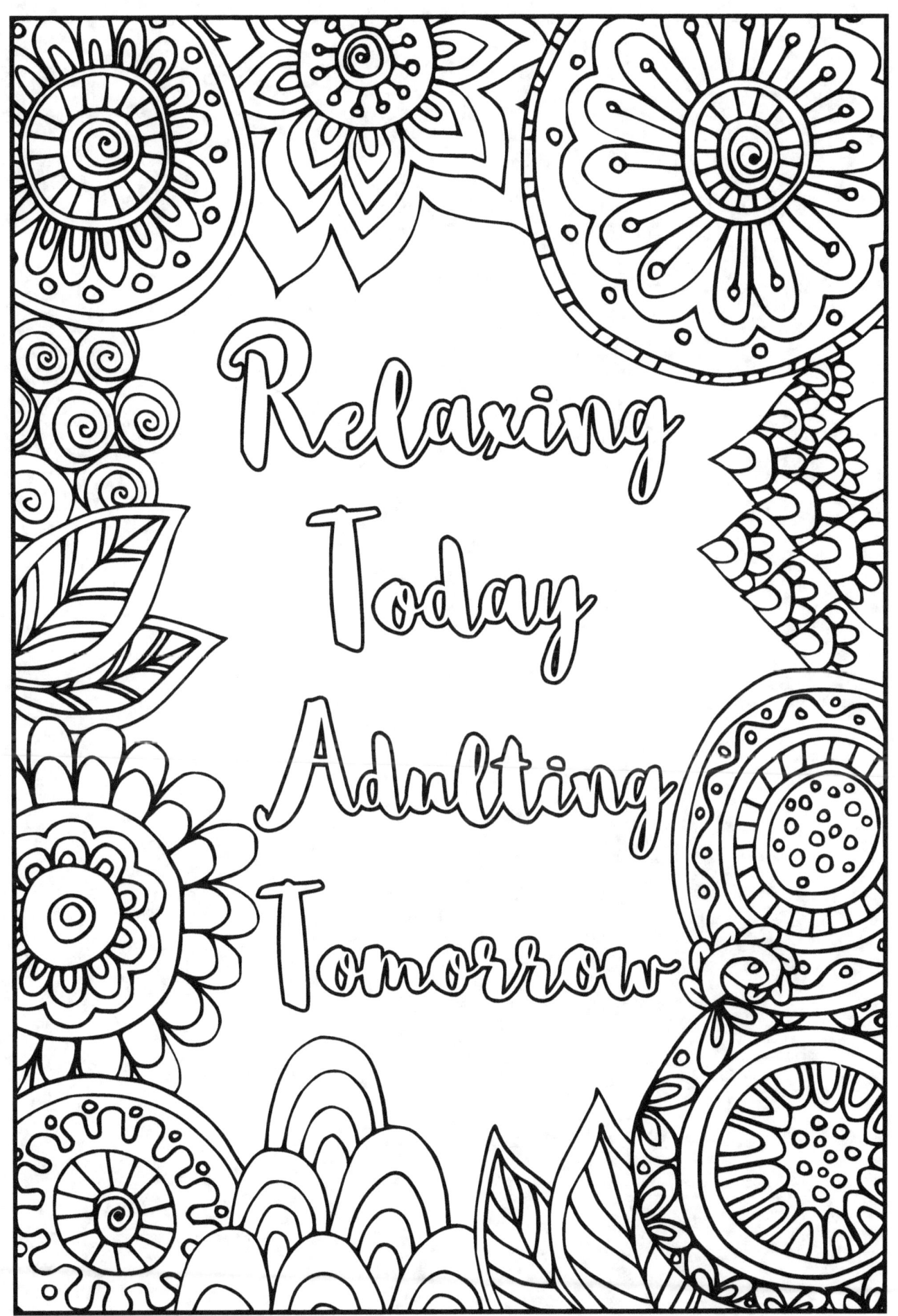

Relaxing Today Adulting Tomorrow

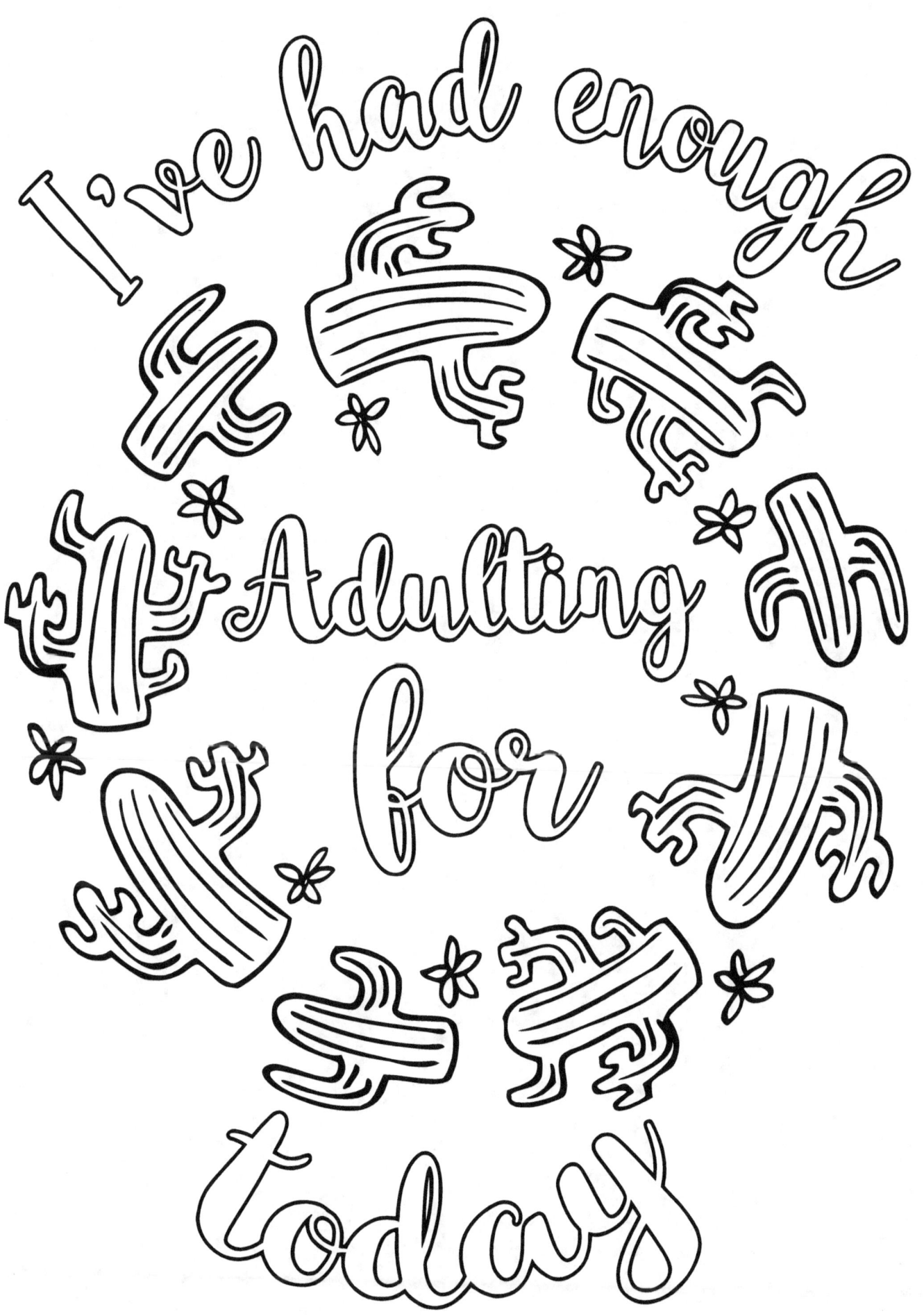

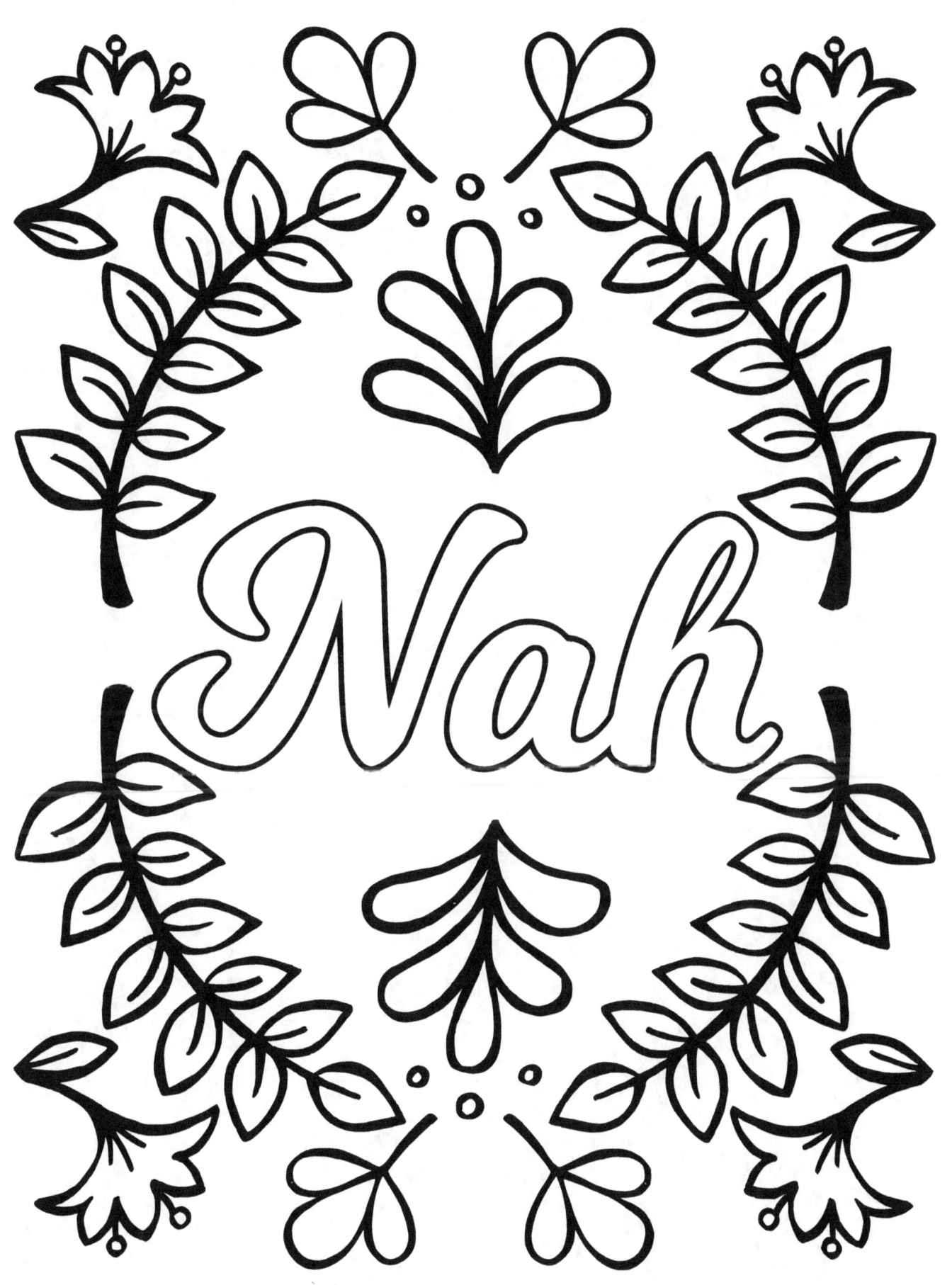

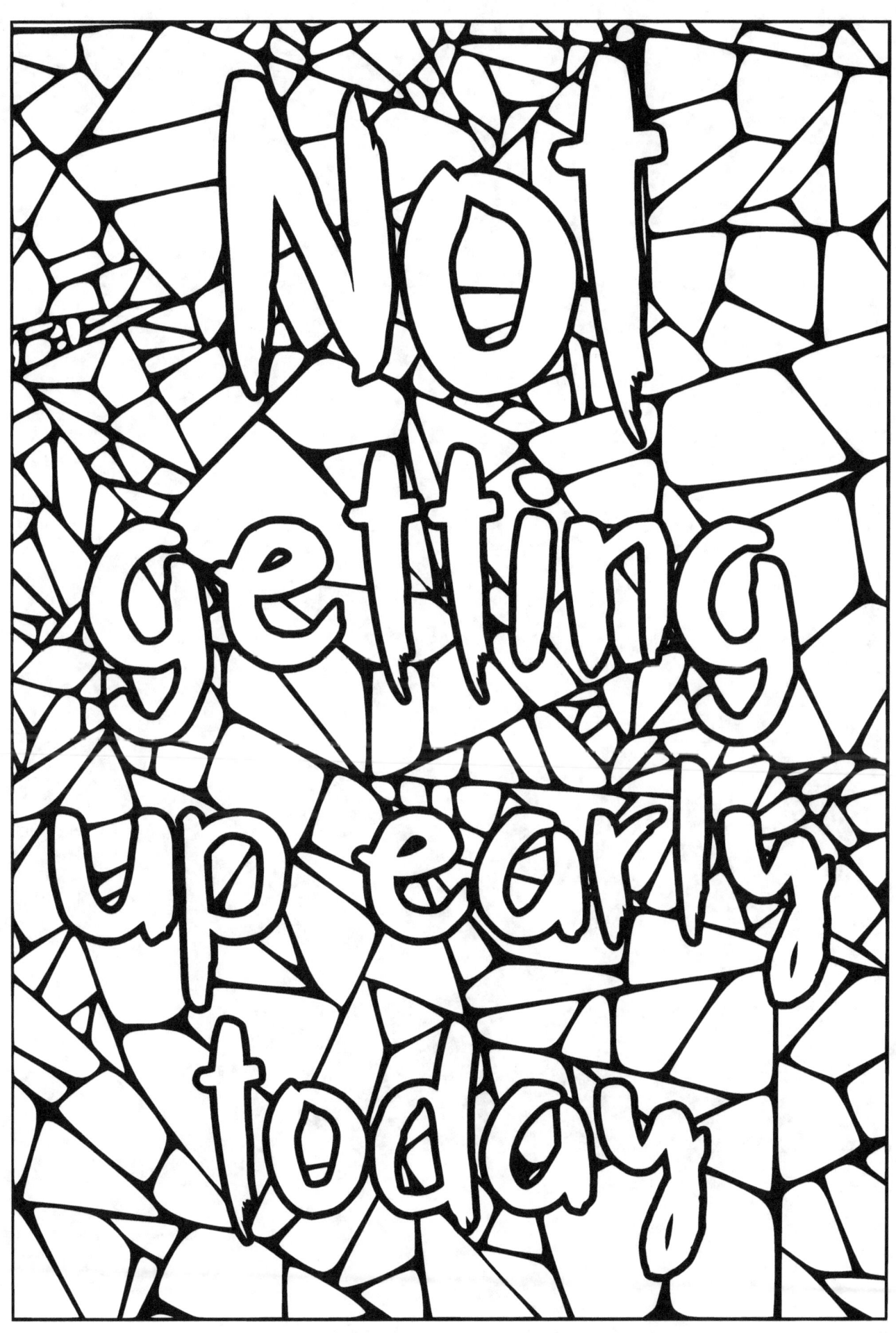

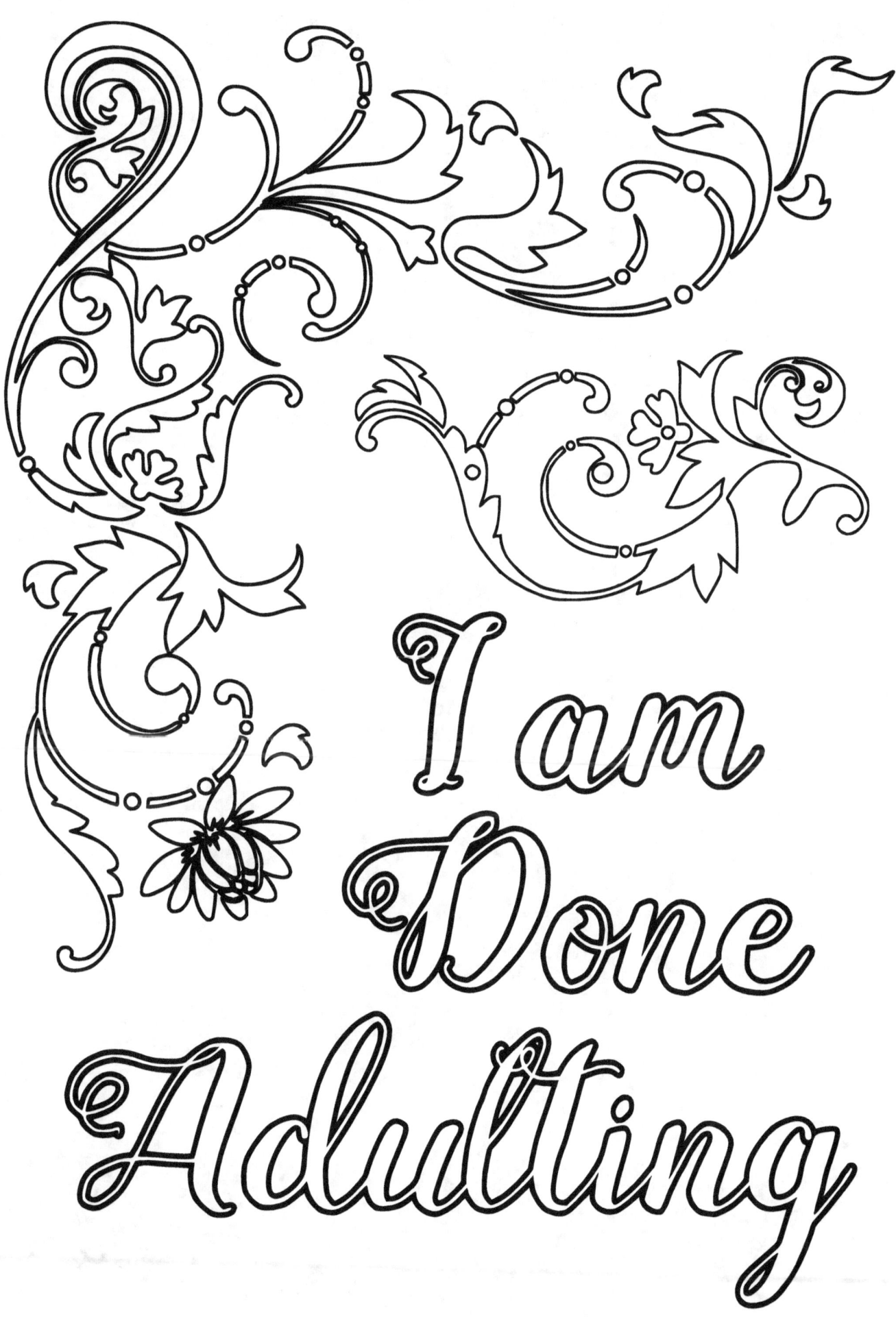

I am Done Adulting

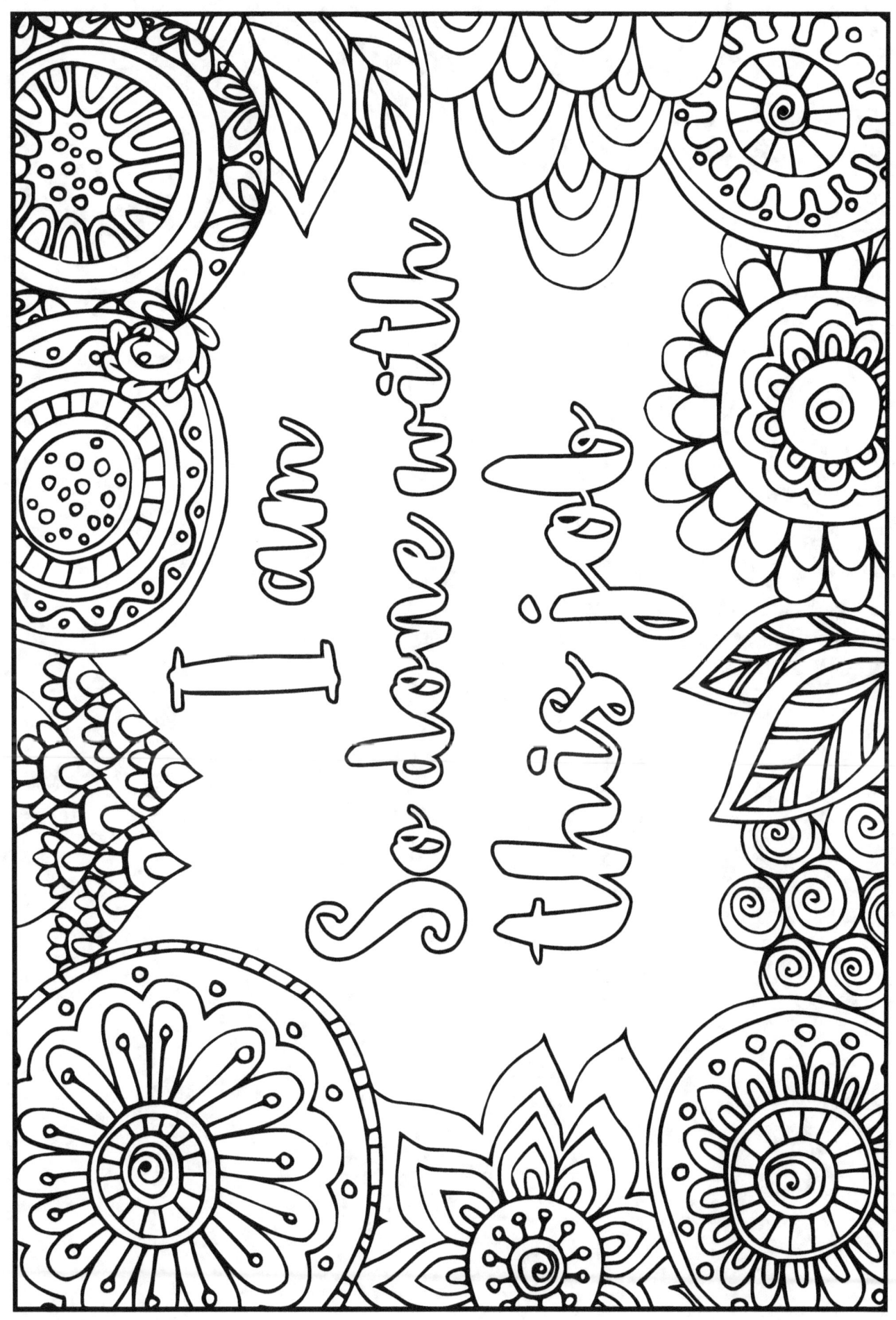

I am
So done with
this job

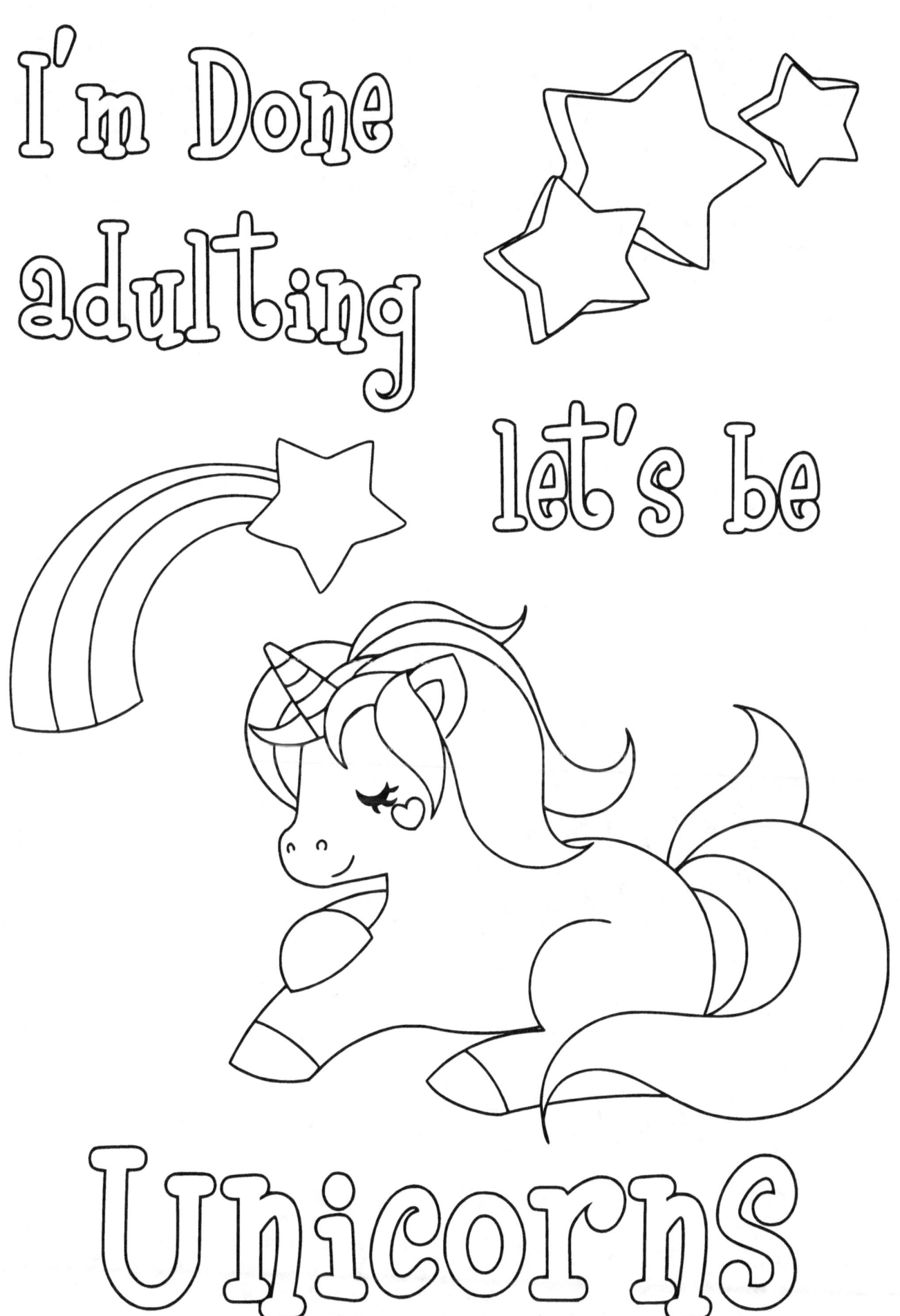

I'm Done adulting let's be Unicorns

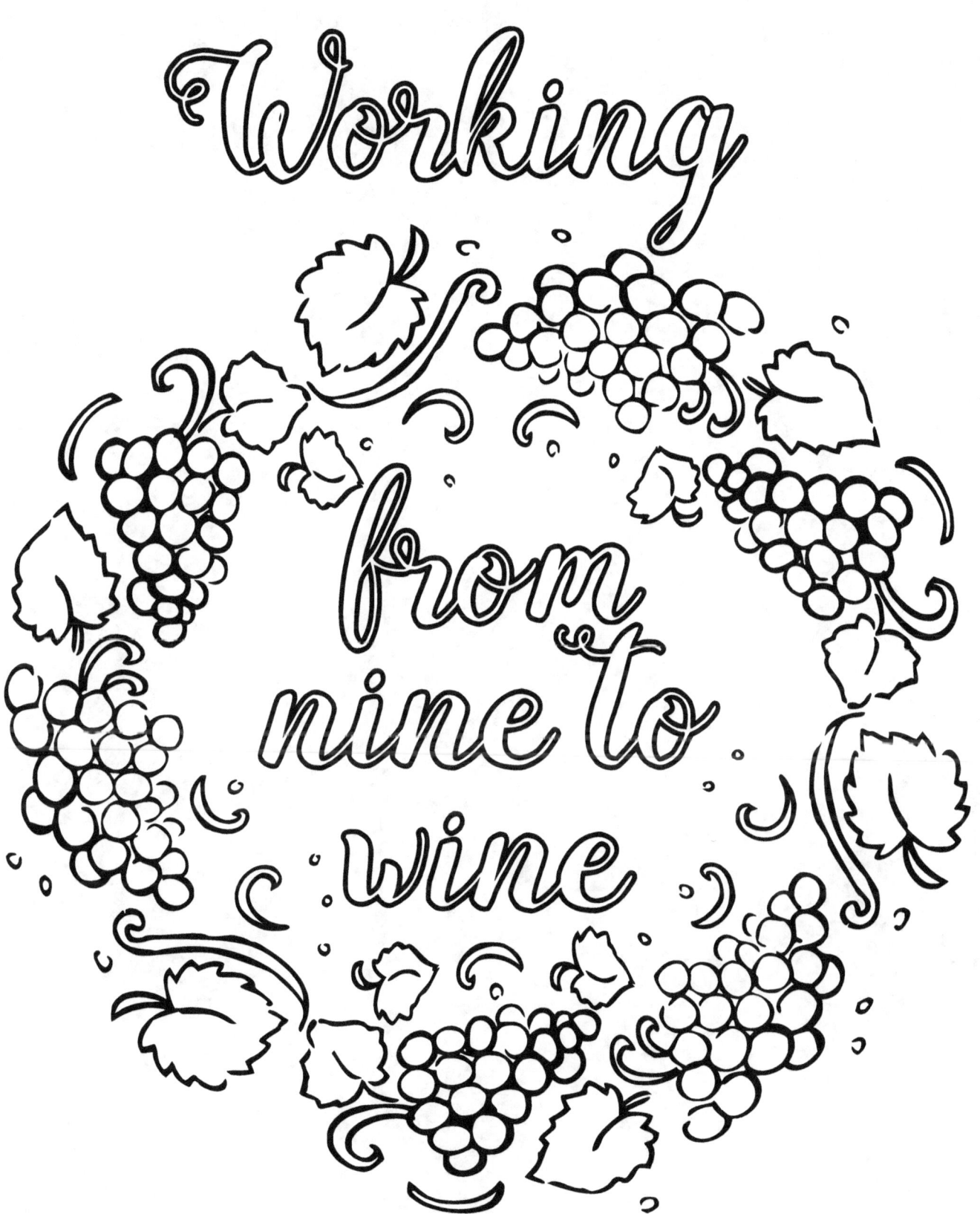

Working from nine to wine

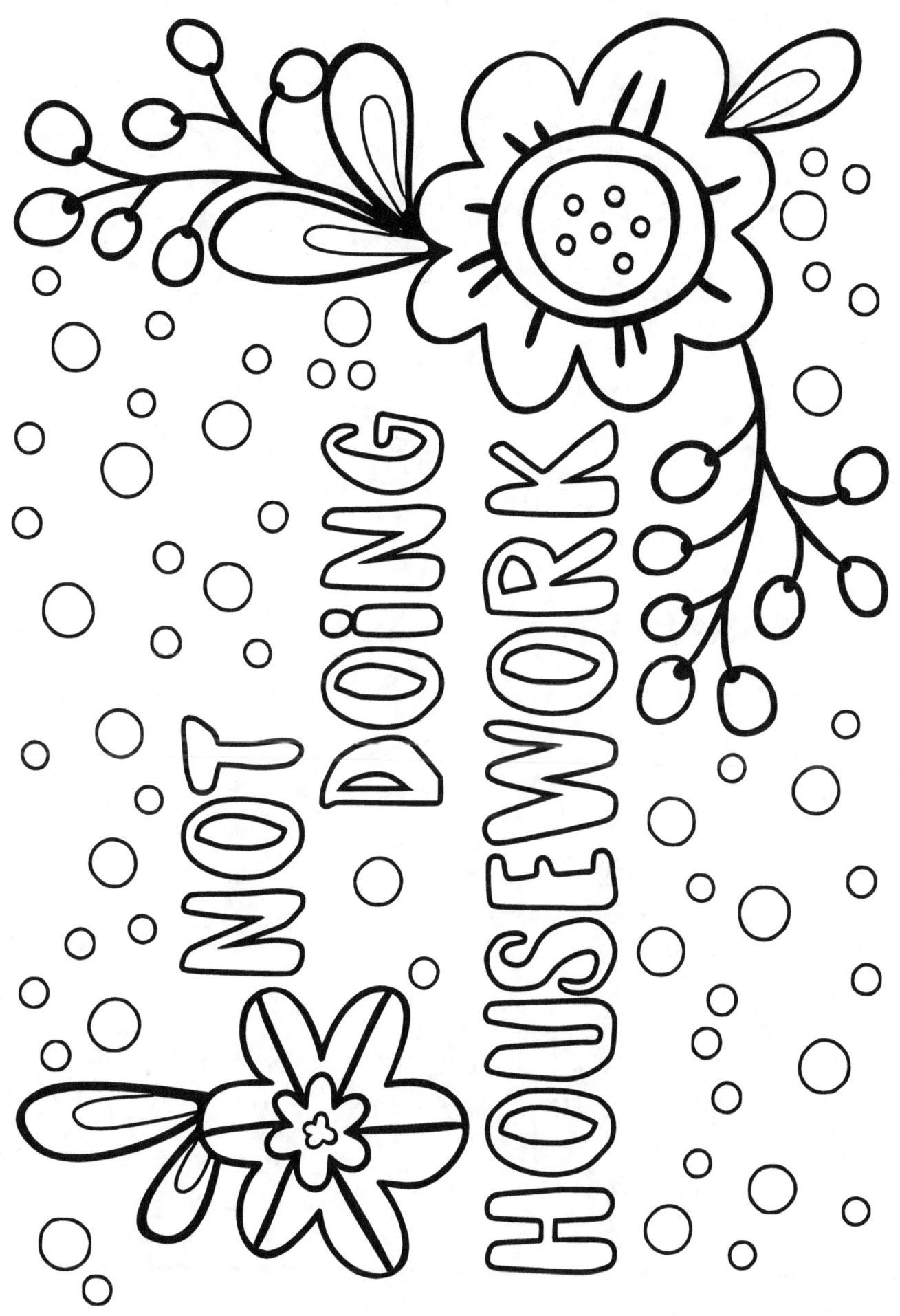

NOT DOING HOUSEWORK

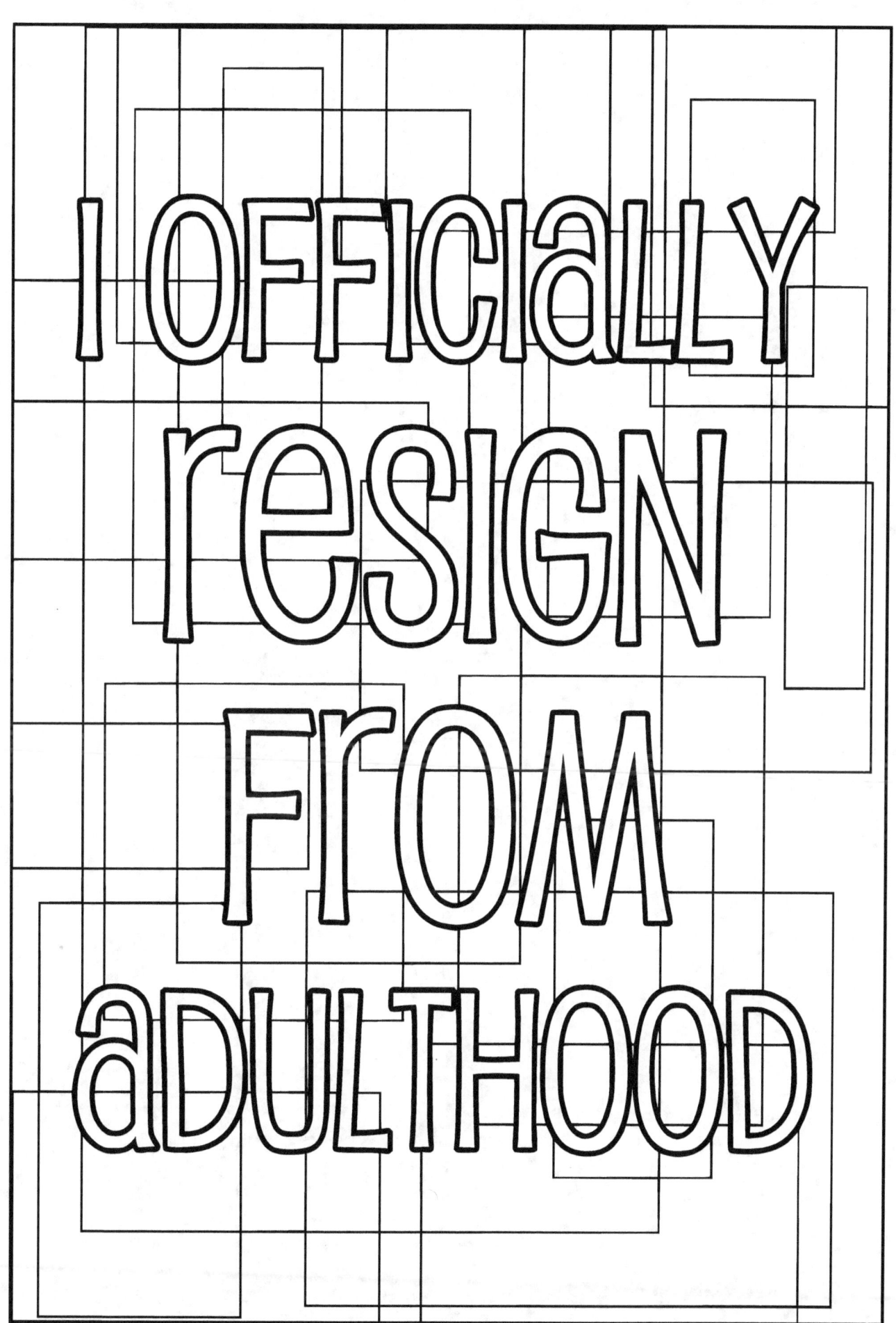

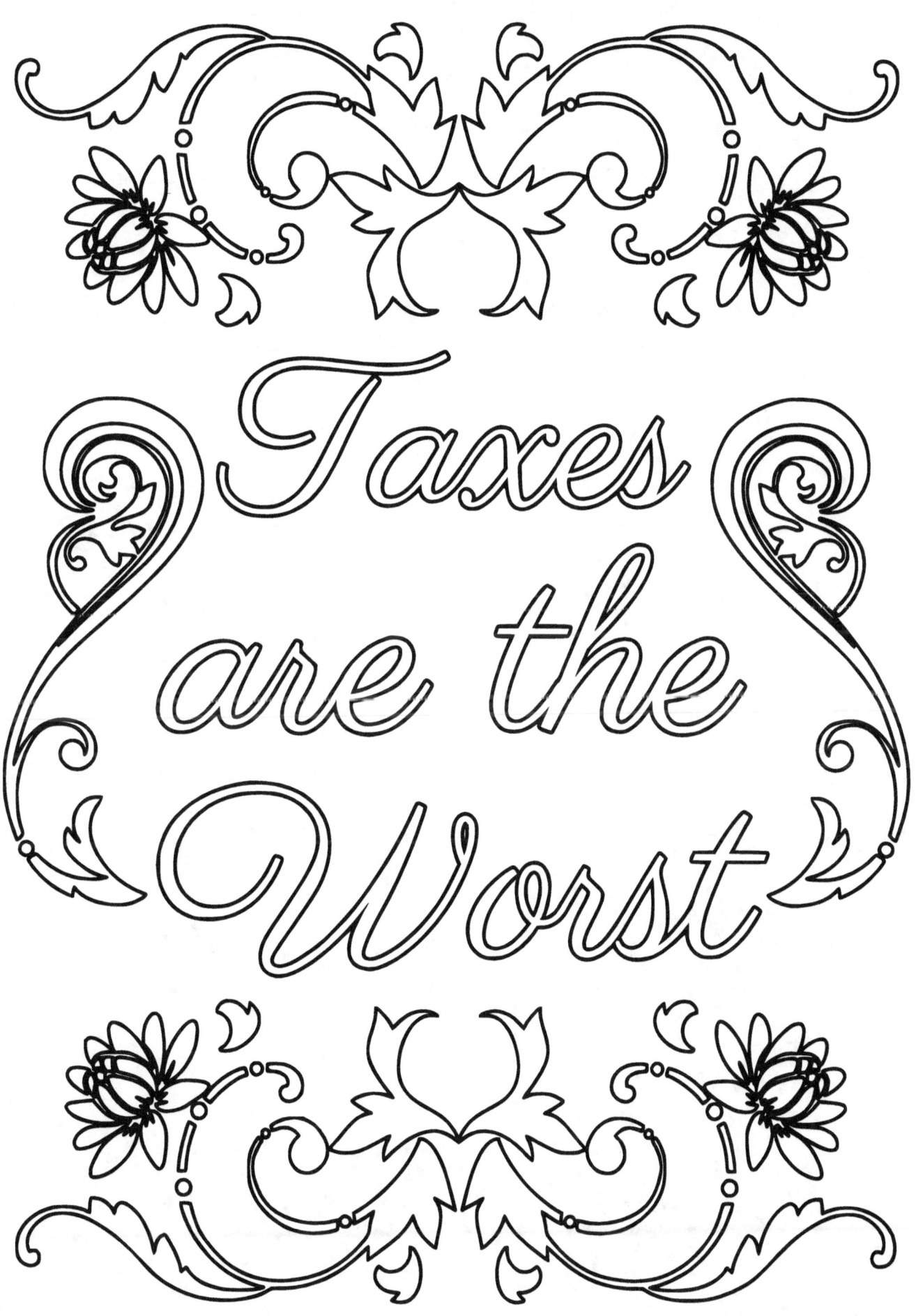

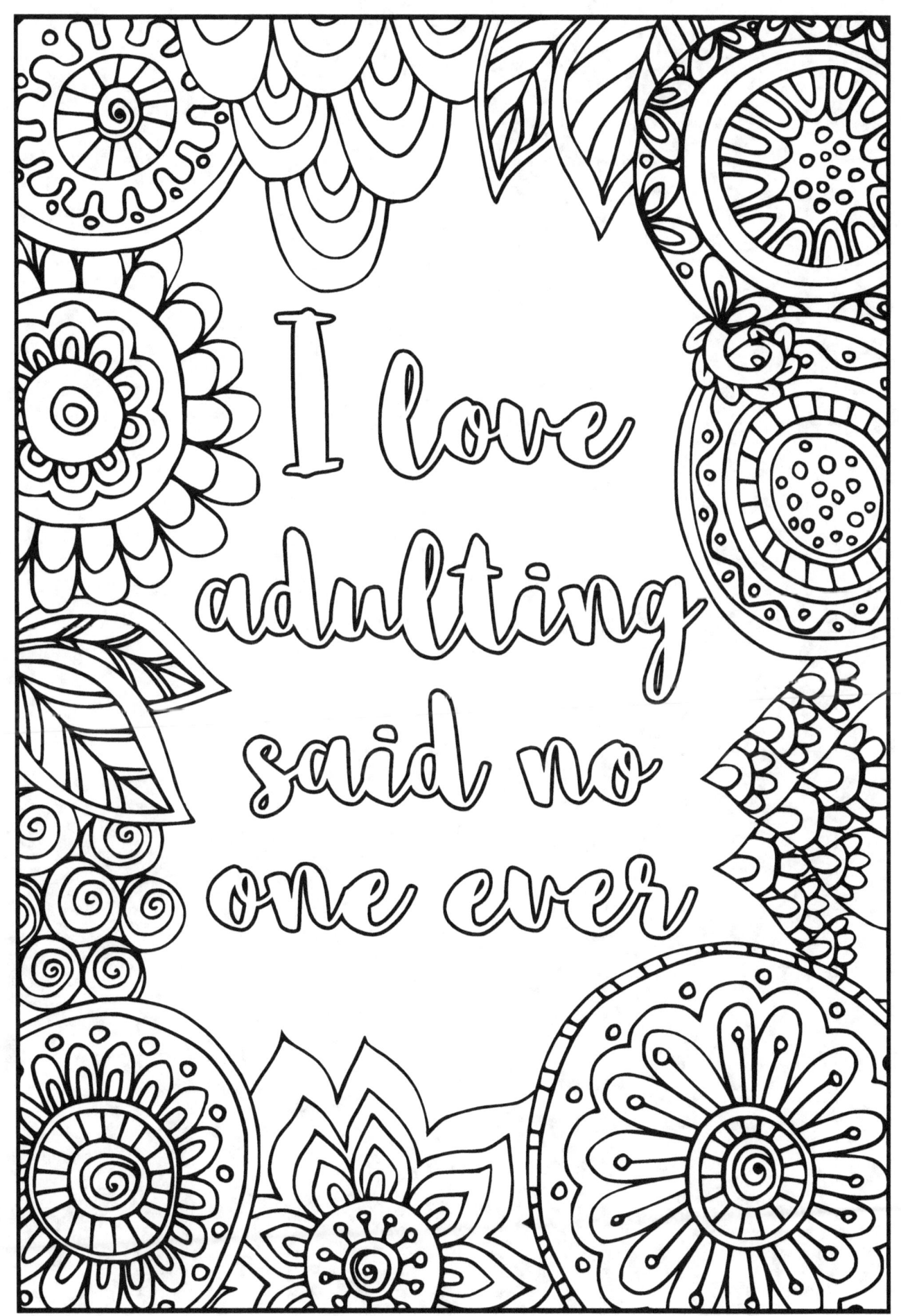

I love adulting said no one ever

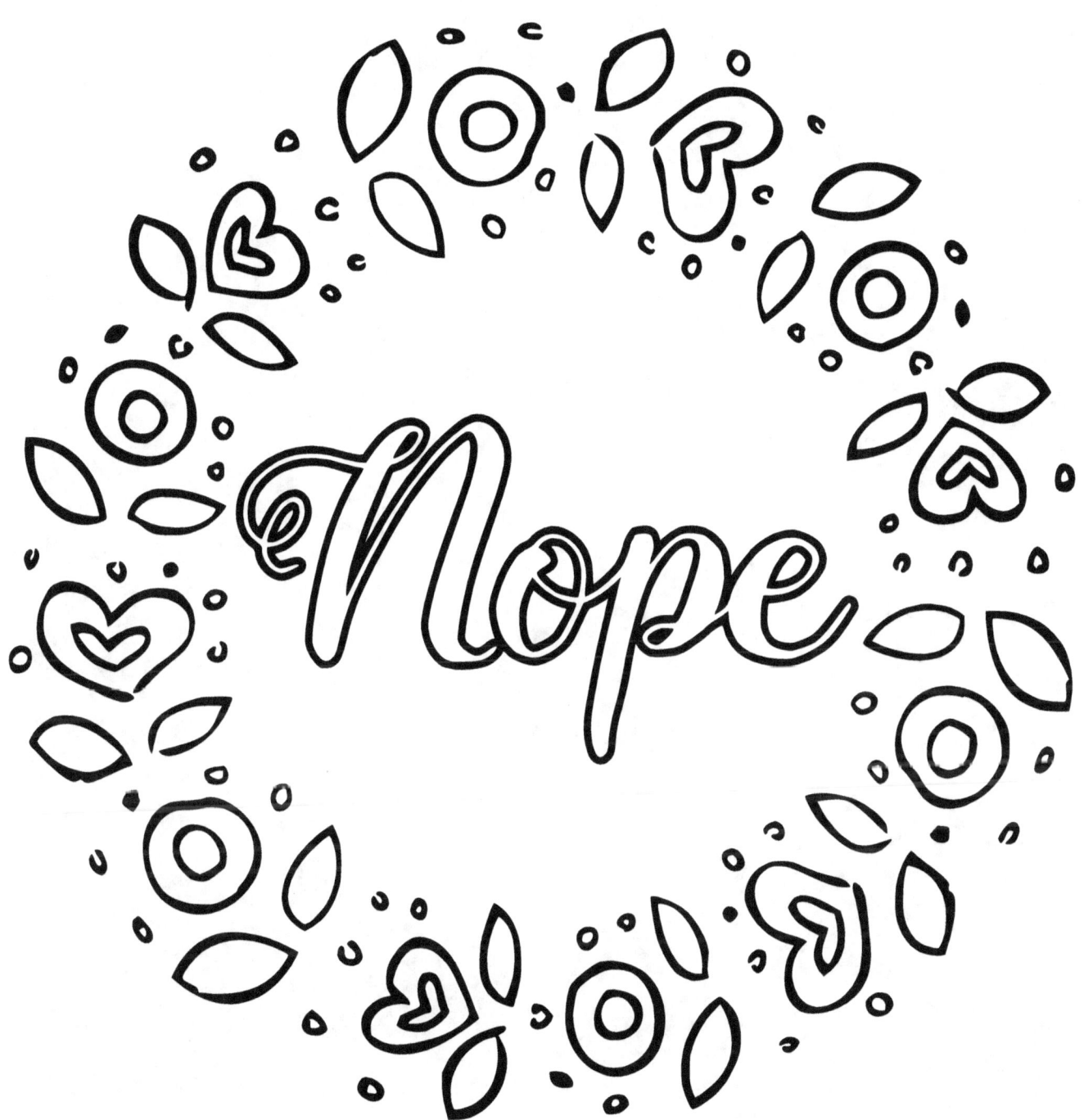

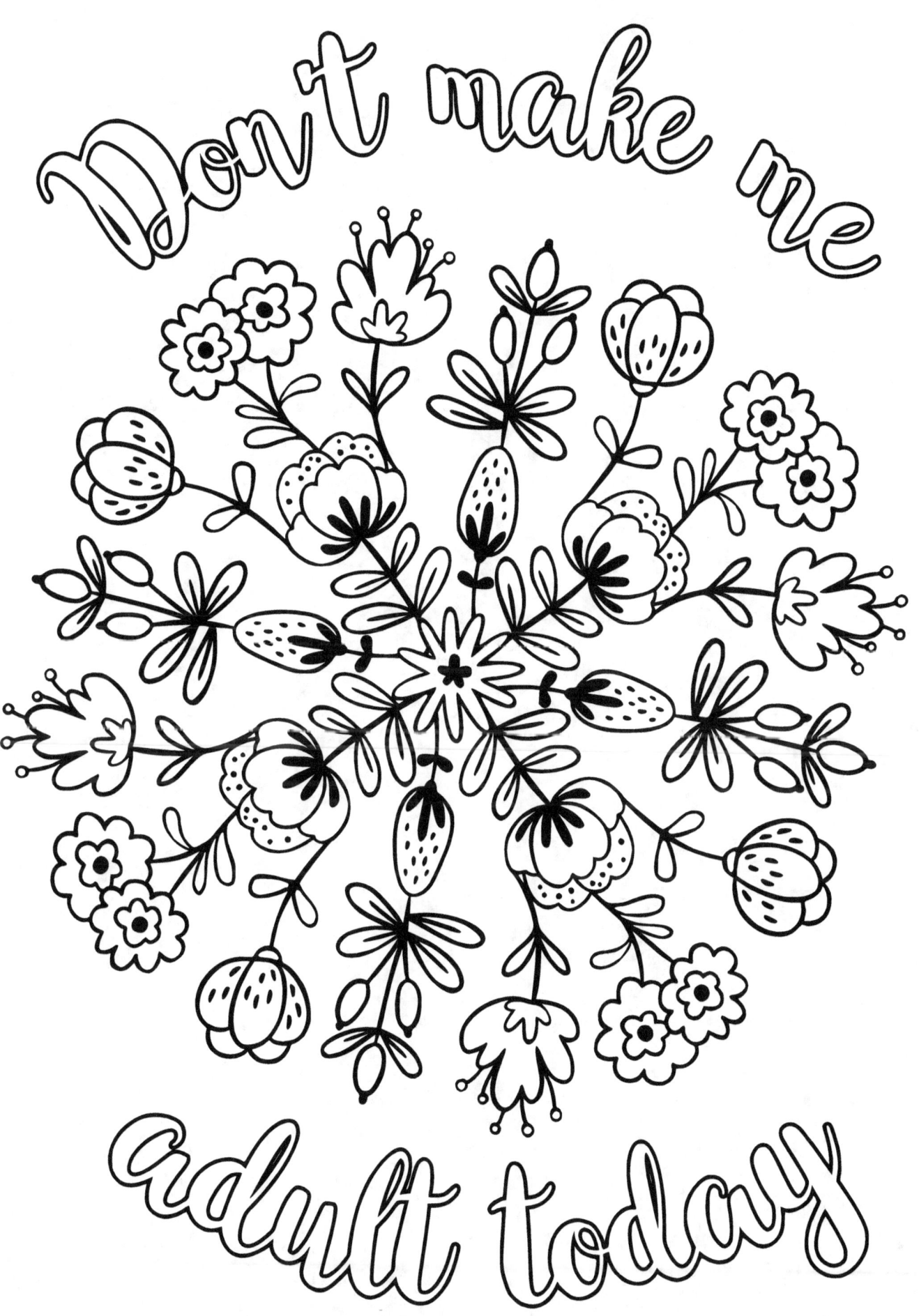

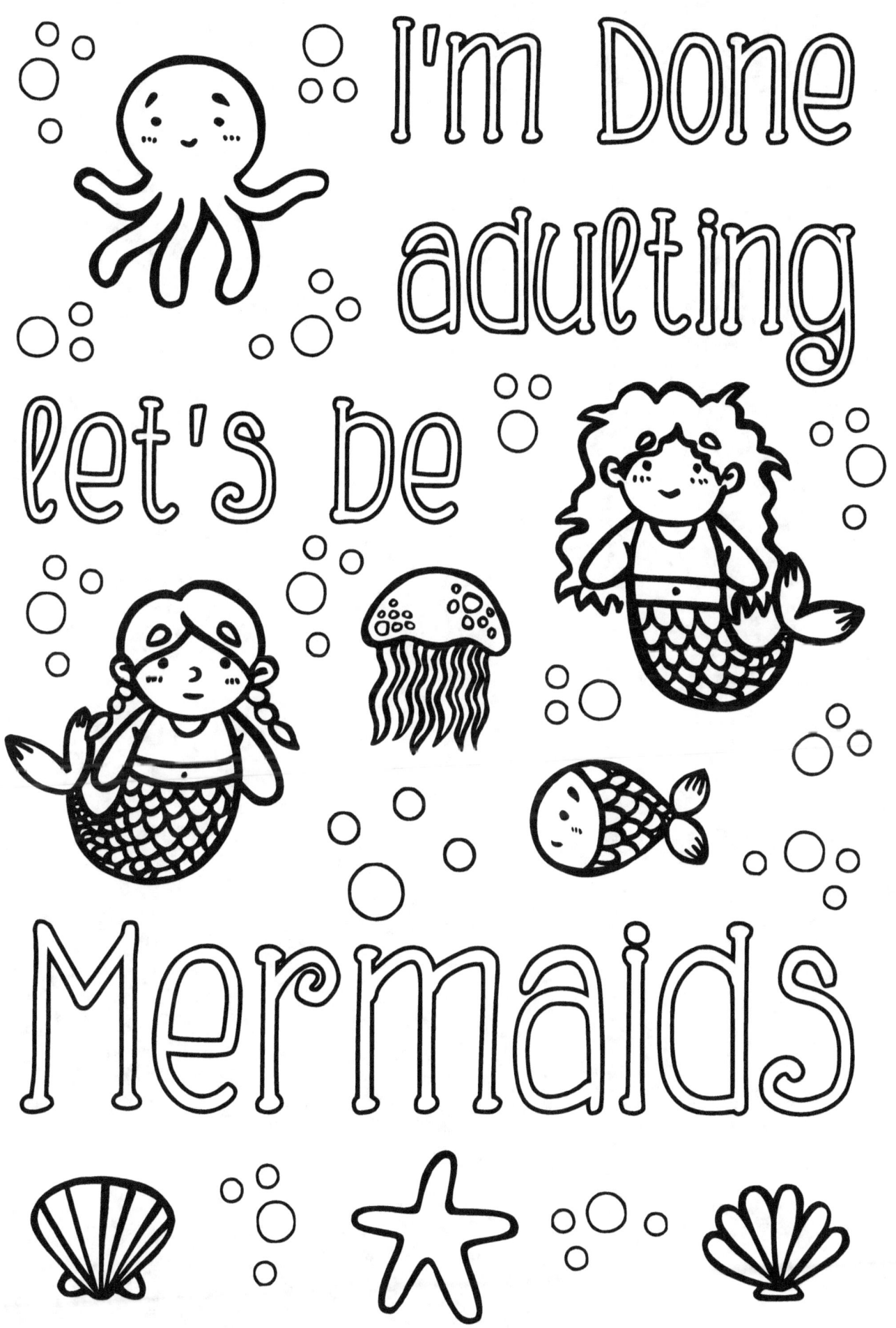

I'm Done
adulting
let's be
Mermaids

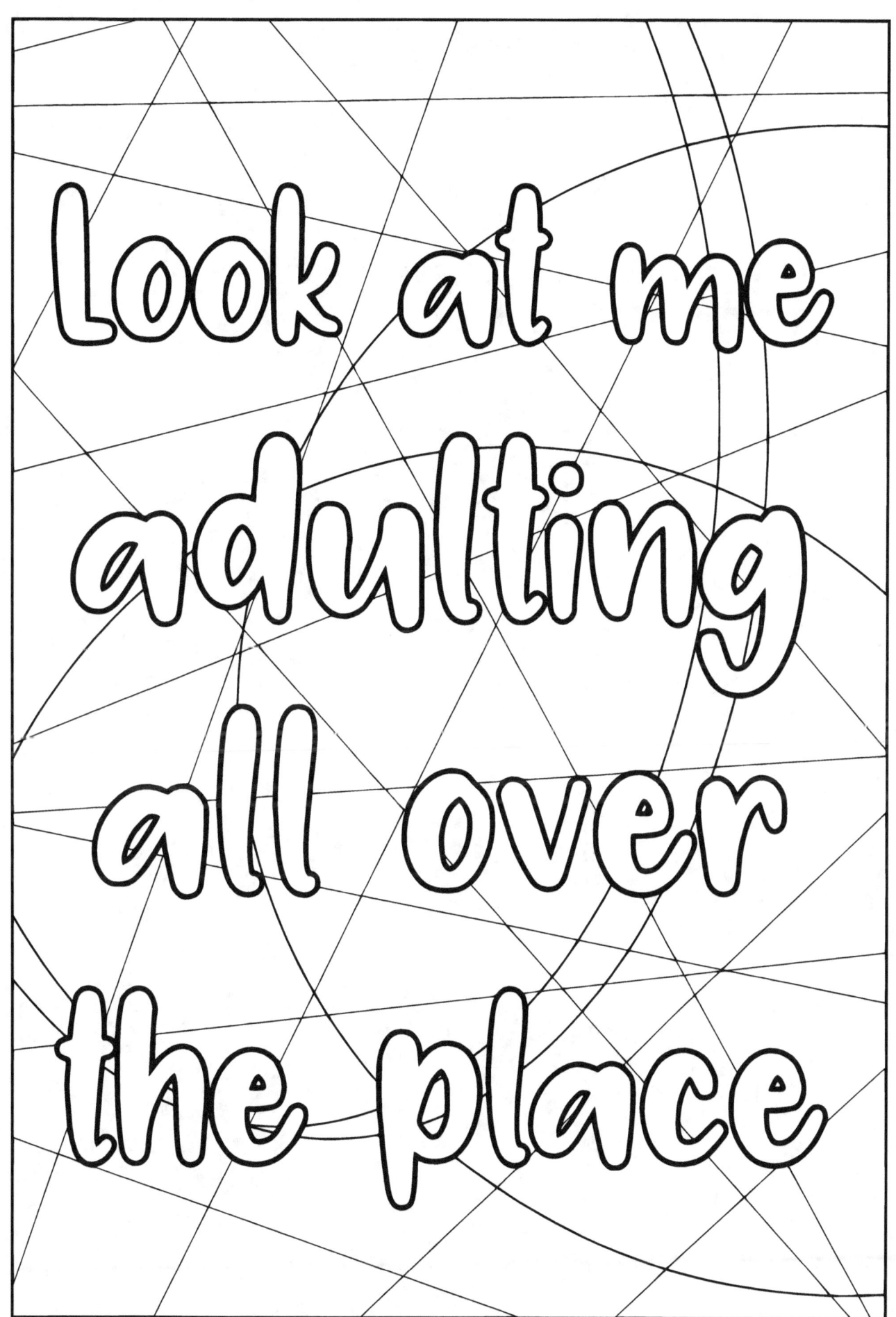

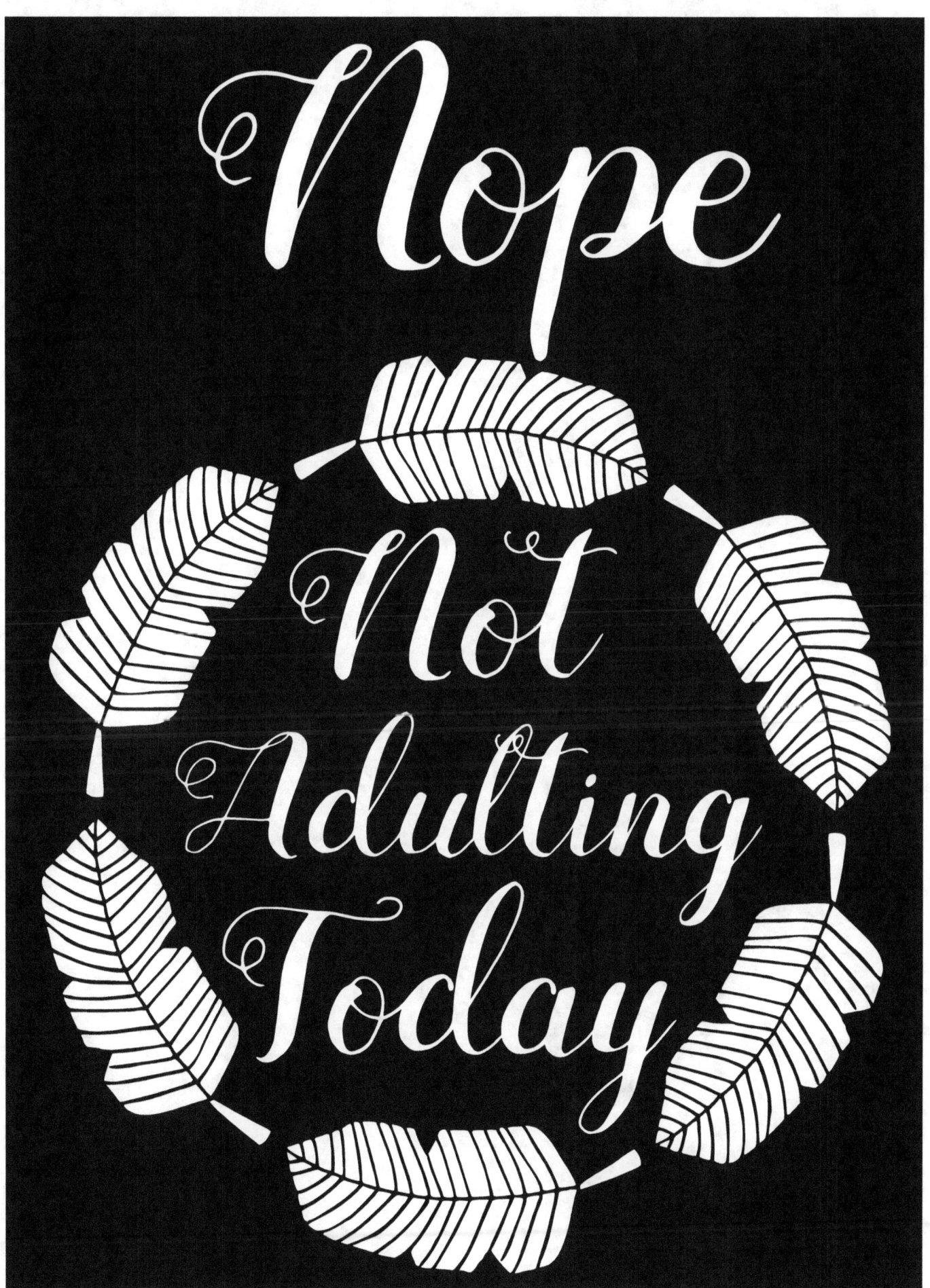

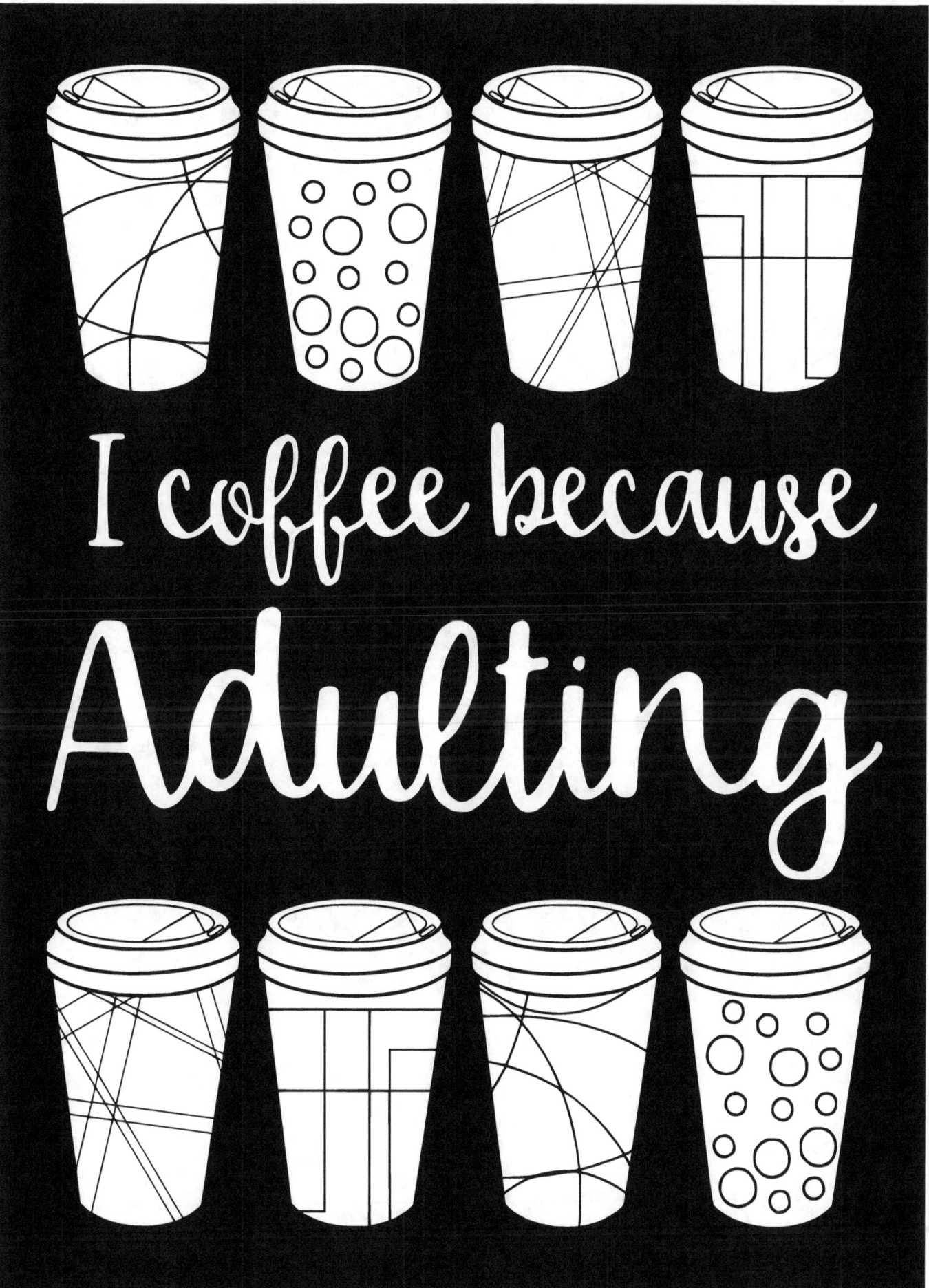

I coffee because Adulting

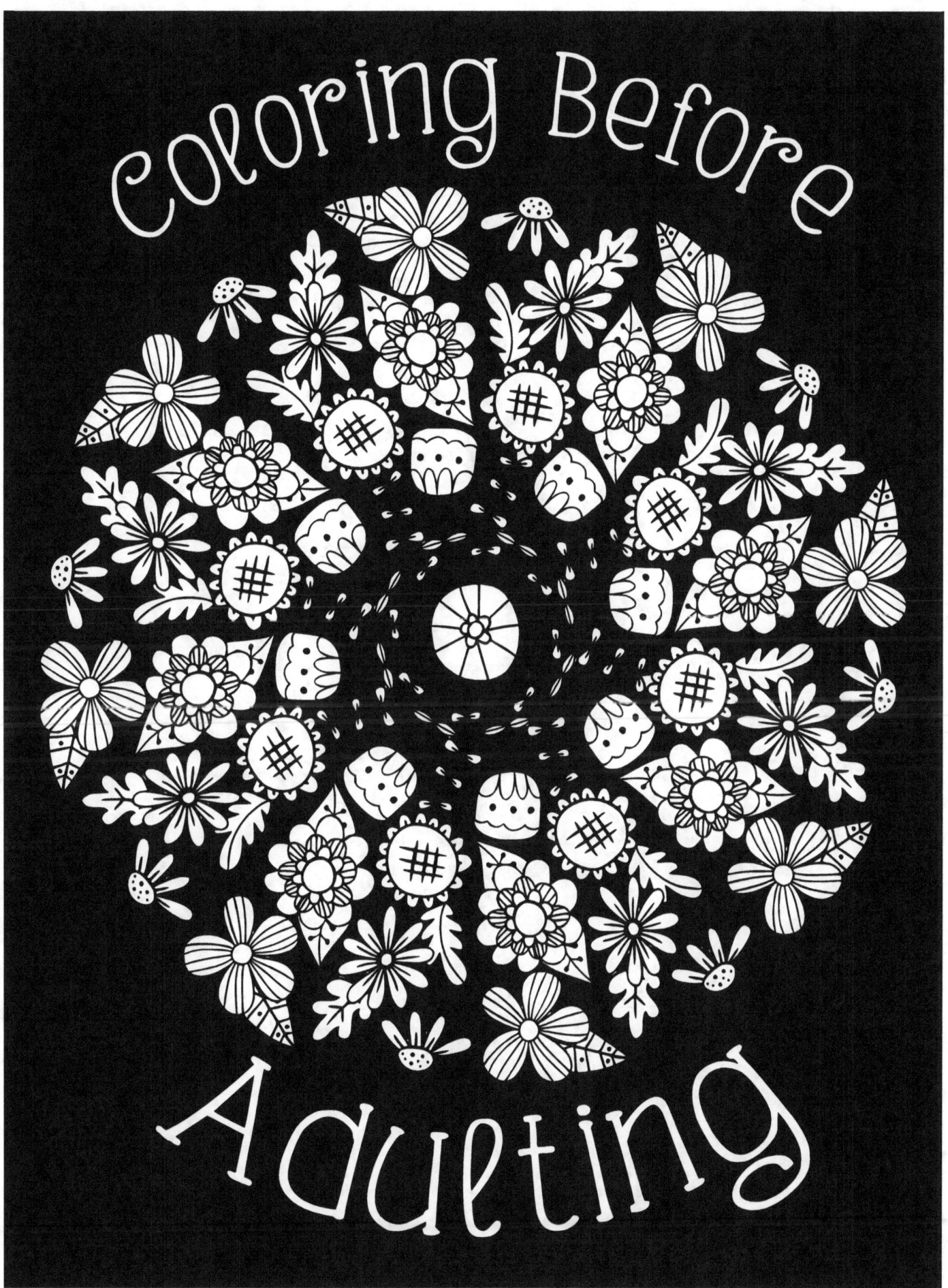

Coloring Before Adulting

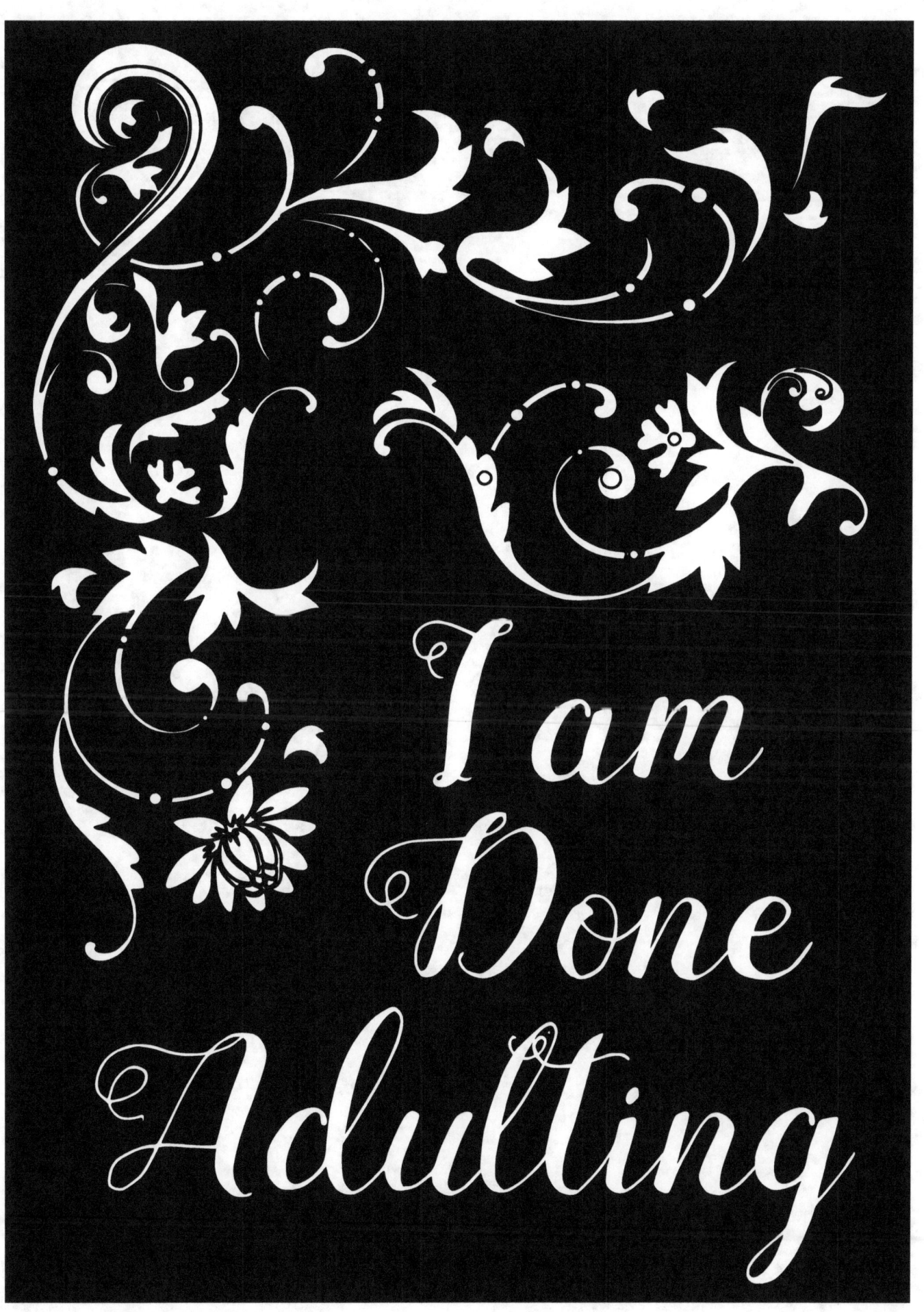

I am Done Adulting

I'm Done adulting let's be Unicorns

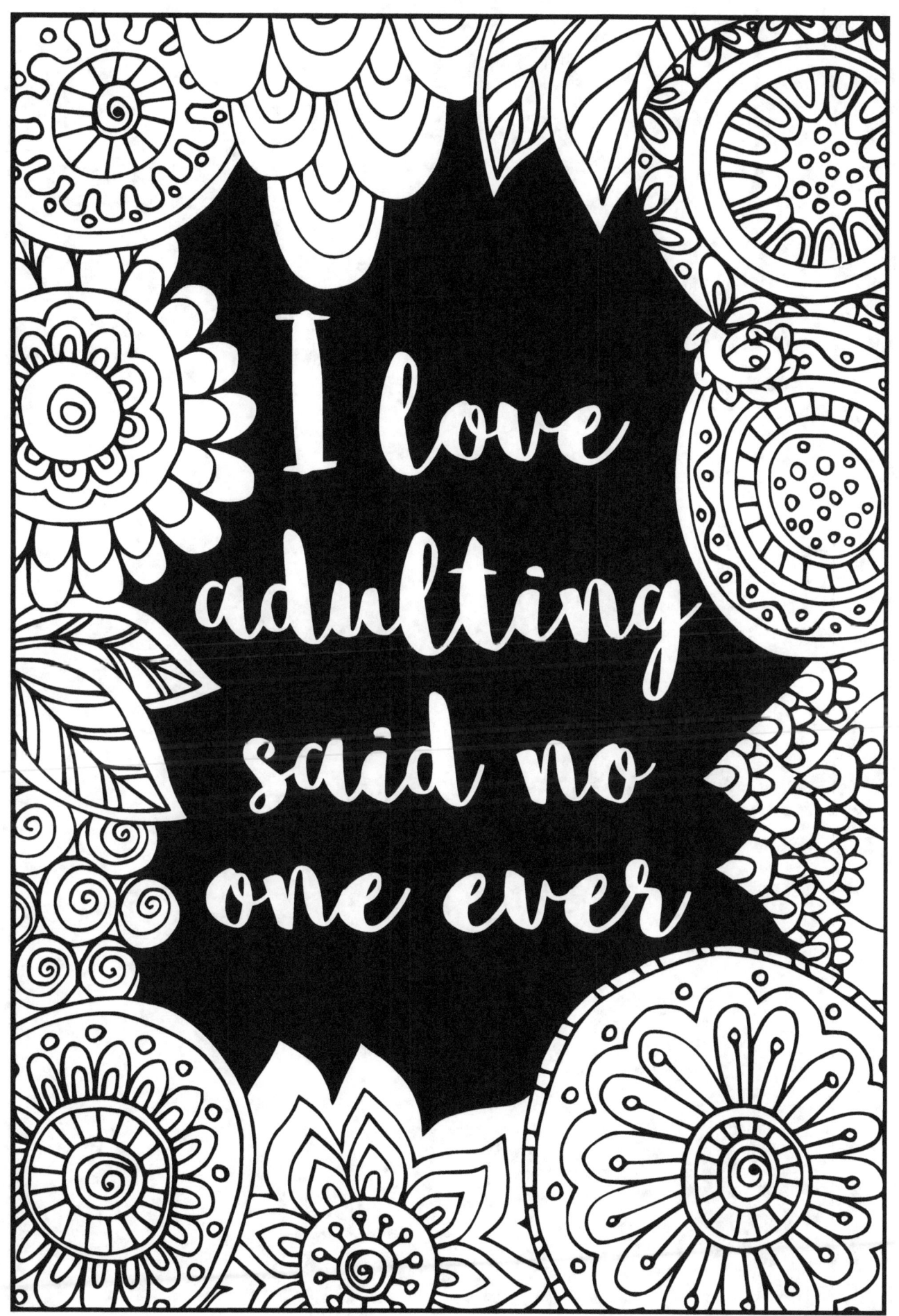

I love adulting said no one ever

SPREAD THE WORD

Please take a moment to leave a
review for this book on Amazon

THIS BOOK IS ALSO AVAILABLE
IN A SWEARY VERSION

For those adulting moments when
only swearing will do.
Makes a perfect gift for your
sweary friends, too!

Check out my Facebook page
for my other books, electronic downloads,
apparel, totes, stickers, posters,
notebooks, and more!

Facebook.com/PardonMyFrenchColoring